DREAMWEAVER MX

NICK VANDOME

BARNES
&NOBLE
BOOKS
NEW YORK

In easy steps is an imprint of Computer Step
Southfield Road . Southam
Warwickshire CV47 0FB . United Kingdom
www.ineasysteps.com

This edition published for Barnes & Noble Books, New York
FOR SALE IN THE USA ONLY
www.bn.com

Notice of Liability
Every effort has been made to ensure that this book contains
accurate and current information. However, Computer Step and the
author shall not be liable for any loss or damage suffered by readers
as a result of any information contained herein.

Trademarks
Dreamweaver® is a registered trademark of Macromedia, Inc. All
other trademarks are acknowledged as belonging to their respective
companies.

Printed and bound in the United Kingdom

ISBN 0-7607-4775-X

Contents

Introducing Dreamweaver

Dreamweaver is a powerful Web authoring tool that can be used to create highly professional websites. This chapter looks at obtaining and installing the program and explains some of the features that will enable you to start working at creating Web pages.

Covers

Chapter One

About Dreamweaver

In the early days of Web design, the code used to create Web pages was inputted manually. This required the page designers to have a reasonable amount of knowledge of this code, HyperText Markup Language (HTML). While this is not a full-blown computer language and it can be learned reasonably quickly, it can be a time-consuming business to create complicated Web pages in this fashion.

Before you start creating Web pages, it is a good idea to learn the basics of HTML, either with a book or a course. There are numerous training courses and night-classes in HTML coding.

The next development in Web design software was the introduction of HTML editors. These are programs that help make the process of creating HTML code quicker and easier by giving the author shortcuts for adding the elements that make up the coded page. However, this still requires a good basic knowledge of HTML: it makes the process quicker for the experienced designer but it does not help the novice much.

The big breakthrough in Web design software, and one that introduced a huge new audience to the joys of Web design, was the introduction of WYSIWYG programs. This stands for What You See Is What You Get and they enable people to design their own Web pages without having to even be aware of the existence of HTML. They work in a similar way to a word processing or a desktop publishing program: what you layout on the screen is what the end user will see on their computer. With these programs, the HTML is still present (and you can edit it manually if you desire) but it is all generated automatically by the program in the background.

Even when you are using a WYSIWYG Web authoring program, it is still important to follow the basics of good Web design.

Dreamweaver is a WYSIWYG Web authoring program that provides an effective interface for quickly creating high quality Web pages. In addition, it contains a range of powerful tools for incorporating the latest Web design elements into sites to give them a highly professional look. Overall, Dreamweaver is an ideal program for anyone involved in designing websites: its combination of simplicity and power makes it an excellent choice for the novice and professional alike. For the experienced Web designer, Dreamweaver MX also has improved functions for creating dynamic Web pages – these are used in conjunction with databases and can change depending on the user's requirements.

Obtaining Dreamweaver

Dreamweaver is produced by Macromedia, one of the market leaders in Web design software. They produce a wide range of products for incorporating the latest Web design technology, including programs such as Flash and Fireworks, and Dreamweaver allows easy integration with other Macromedia products, to provide the greatest power and flexibility for the least amount of effort.

Dreamweaver can be obtained from most good software suppliers, although in some cases it may have to be ordered. Alternatively it can be downloaded directly from the Dreamweaver page on the Macromedia site at `www.macromedia.com/software/dreamweaver/`:

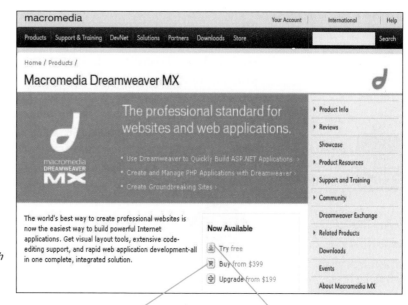

For image editing, Dreamweaver is very closely integrated with Fireworks MX, also from Macromedia.

On the Dreamweaver page, click Buy to begin downloading the program or to order the boxed version

Click Try to obtain a 30-day, fully functioning, trial version of Dreamweaver. (To purchase the retail version while you are using the trial version, click on the Buy Now button on the program's startup window.)

Installing Dreamweaver

To run Dreamweaver MX on Windows, you need the following:

- *Pentium II Processor 300 MHz or faster*
- *Windows 98, Me, 2000, NT (Service Pack) or XP*
- *96 Mb of memory (128 Mb recommended)*
- *275 Mb of disc space*
- *800 x 600 256-color monitor*
- *Version 4.0 or later of Netscape Navigator or Microsoft Internet Explorer*
- *CD-ROM drive*

To run Dreamweaver MX on the Mac, you need the following:

- *Power Macintosh Processor G3 or higher*
- *Mac OS 9.1 or above*

The rest of the requirements are the same as in the above tip.

Before installing Dreamweaver, either by downloading it from the Macromedia site or from a retail CD-ROM, it is necessary to ensure that your computer is capable of running the program to its full capacity. Due to some of the multimedia elements that can be incorporated into Dreamweaver it is important that the requirements on the left are met, otherwise you may encounter problems when trying to utilize certain parts of the program.

When you begin to install Dreamweaver, a screen will appear informing you that the installation process is about to begin. Select Next to continue through the steps of the installation process. This will include the automatic creation of a folder into which all of the Dreamweaver files will be placed. Unless you have a good reason not to, leave this default folder as the one chosen by the program.

Once the installation process has been completed, the best way to access Dreamweaver is to place a shortcut (PC) or alias (Mac) on your desktop. To create a desktop shortcut on a PC, locate the program in its application folder, right-click on it and drag it onto the desktop. Release the icon and select Create Shortcut(s) Here from the menu. To create a desktop shortcut on a Mac, select the item, then select File>Make Alias from the Menu bar. Once the alias has been created, you can move it to where you want it. The following icon should then be visible on the desktop:

Shortcut to Dreamweaver
Shortcut
1 KB

If you have created a shortcut or alias on your desktop, double-click on this icon to launch Dreamweaver. This icon can also be added to the Taskbar (Windows) or the Dock (Mac OS X) for quick access by clicking on it once.

Layout options

When Dreamweaver MX is first launched you are presented with three options for how you would like the workspace laid out. These are:

- Dreamweaver MX Workspace, which is the graphical workspace

- HomeSite/Coder-Style, which is the workspace for creating HTML code manually

- Dreamweaver 4 Workspace, which replicates the workspace of the previous version of the program

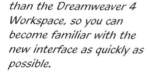

It is a good idea to use the Dreamweaver MX Workspace initially rather than the Dreamweaver 4 Workspace, so you can become familiar with the new interface as quickly as possible.

When Dreamweaver is launched, click on one of the workspace options

2 Click OK

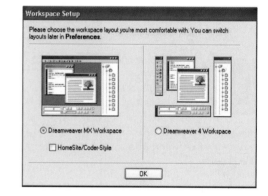

Changing the workspace

It is possible to change the workspace at any time:

Changes to the workspace only take effect once the program has been closed down and then opened again.

Select Edit> Preferences from the Menu bar and select the General category

2 Click on Change Workspace and select the options as above. Click OK

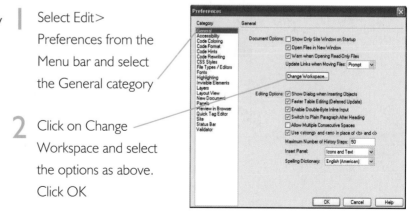

Workspaces

Dreamweaver MX Workspace (Windows)

This is the default workspace and it enables you to create WYSIWYG Web pages by placing graphical and textual elements in the workspace, knowing that this is how they should appear in a browser. The Dreamweaver MX Workspace also has options for entering HTML code by hand and even viewing the code and the graphical interface simultaneously. The main elements of the Dreamweaver MX Workspace are:

The Mac version only has the standard Dreamweaver MX Workspace which is virtually identical to the Windows version on this page.

The icon at the right of the View options is for displaying data on dynamic Web pages. For more information on this, see Chapter Ten.

Insert Panel (often used elements)   Code View   Code and Design View   Design View

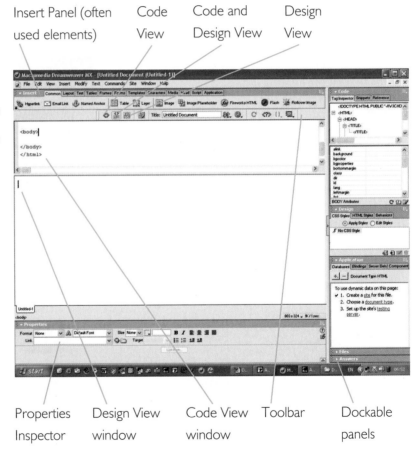

Properties Inspector   Design View window   Code View window   Toolbar   Dockable panels

HomeSite/Coder-Style Workspace (Windows only)

This is the workspace for people who want to work primarily with handwritten HTML code. It incorporates a previously separate HTML editor, HomeSite, into Dreamweaver MX so that hand coders can now enjoy the same power and versatility as those working with the graphical interface. In the HomeSite/Coder-Style Workspace, the same elements can be inserted as with the Dreamweaver MX Workspace, but the default is Code View. The layout is optimized to make HomeSite users feel comfortable in a familiar environment. The main elements of the HomeSite/Coder-Style Workspace are:

The Mac version does not have the HomeSite/ Coder-Style Workspace option. If you want to create HTML code manually the recommended editor is BBEdit, which integrates closely with the Mac version of Dreamweaver MX.

Dockable panels

Insert panel (often used elements)

View (Code, Code and Design and Design) icons – see facing page

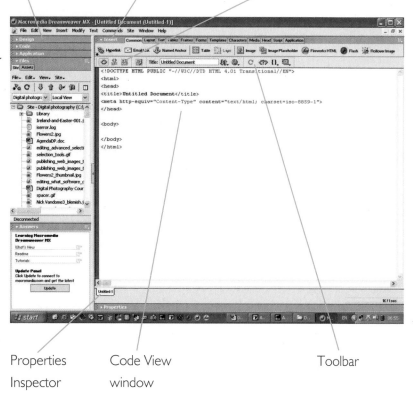

Properties Inspector

Code View window

Toolbar

Preferences

Dreamweaver offers extensive options for the way the program looks and operates. These are located in the Preferences menu. The preferences can be used to change the way the program and its elements appear, and also to change the way certain tasks are performed. There are dozens of these preferences, which cover specific elements of the program, and these will be covered in the relevant chapters. However, there are some preferences that are useful to look at before you start using Dreamweaver.

Take some time to look at the available preferences in Dreamweaver. Although you will not use all of them at this point, it is a good way to get a feel for the type of thing you can change within the program.

Panels

These preferences can be used to select which panel you want to have displayed and which items you want included in the Launcher (see the facing page):

Open the Preferences window. Click entries here to show or hide panels

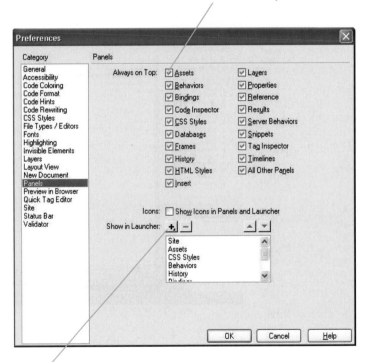

Click here to add items to the Launcher

Insert panel

This option is contained within the General preference options and can be used to determine how the information in the Insert panel is displayed. Since this is one of the most commonly used panels, it is worthwhile having it set up the way that you want:

If the Insert panel is displayed with icons and text it takes up more room on screen. However, this should be offset against the fact that it can be quicker to locate items within the panel.

Click here to select whether the items in the Insert panel are displayed as icons, text or both

Launcher

The Launcher can be displayed on the Status Bar and it provides quick access to the most frequently used panels. The Launcher can be displayed by checking on the Show Icons in Panels and Launcher option in the Panels Preferences dialog box shown on the previous page. The items displayed in the Launcher can be edited in the Show in Launcher box in the same dialog box.

The Launcher is displayed on the Status Bar at the bottom right of the Dreamweaver window. Click on an item to access its panel

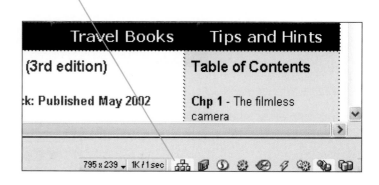

Working with panels

Panels in Dreamweaver MX have replaced the floating palettes in previous versions of the program and they are docked along the side and top of the working environment to allow more space when designing pages. The panels can be selected from the Window menu on the Menu bar. Once panels have been accessed, there are various ways in which to work with them.

Working with panels

Panels are grouped in logical combinations that perform similar general tasks.

To move a panel from its current set, select Group [panel name] With from the panel menu. You can then select another panel set with which to group the selected panel, or select New Panel Group to create it in a set of its own.

Click here to move a panel set

2 Click here to access a panel menu:

Edit...
Duplicate...
Delete
Apply

Use External Editor

New CSS Style...
Edit Style Sheet...
Attach Style Sheet...
Export Style Sheet...
Design Time Style Sheets...

Help

Group CSS Styles with ▶
Rename Panel Group...
Maximize Panel Group
Close Panel Group

3 Click here to expand or collapse a panel

4 To close a panel, click here (Windows) or here (Mac)

▼ Code

Insert panel

The Insert panel is the one that is used most frequently for adding content to Web pages. It contains a number of tabbed categories, each of which can be accessed by clicking on the category's name at the top of the Insert panel:

Select a tabbed category   Click here to add an item

Click here to access additional items for the selected category:

Use the Horizontal Rule option to insert lines to divide items on a page. This can include separating images, text and tables.

Common

This is the default setting and the one that contains some of the most commonly used elements on a Web page, such as hyperlinks, tables, images, multimedia effects and the Tag Chooser for inserting HTML tags.

Layout

This provides options for creating tables and layers and also functions for accessing Layout view which is a method of creating complex tables. For more information about Layout view see Chapter Eight.

Text

This contains buttons for inserting text functions, including bold, italics, preformatted text, headings and lists. Some of these functions are also available on the Text Property Inspector and also from the Text menu on the Menu bar.

Tables

This provides comprehensive features for creating and editing tables. There is also an Insert Table button on the Common tab and also the Layout tab, but the Tables tab has a lot more options, such as including table headers and captions.

Frames

This provides preset options for creating framesets i.e. Web pages that display two or more separate pages at the same time. For more information about this, see Chapter Nine.

Forms

This contains all of the elements that are used in online forms. For more information about this, see Chapter Ten.

Templates

This includes the options for creating template documents, which can be used as a starting point for Web pages with recurring features. The Template tab contains buttons for creating templates and includes editable regions for adding content to the template-based document. Also, Dreamweaver MX has options for creating nested templates and adding repeating editable regions. For more information about this, see Chapter Four.

Characters

This is a collection of buttons for adding special characters to Web pages. These include line breaks, non-breaking spaces, quote marks, dashes, financial symbols, the copyright symbol (©), the registered symbol (®) and the trademark symbol (™).

Flash is a Macromedia program for creating animated effects and interactive elements on a Web page. If it is used carefully it can have a dramatic effect on a website. For more information about Flash, have a look at "Flash MX in easy steps".

Media

This contains options for adding multimedia files such as those created in Flash. There are also options for inserting custom Flash buttons and text. It is also possible to insert Applets and ActiveX objects.

Head

This contains buttons that can be used to insert data into the head section of a Web page. This can include items such as metadata, keywords and descriptions.

Script

This can be used to insert and write scripts such as Javascript.

Application

This can be used to insert elements of a dynamic Web page when using a server technology such as ColdFusion.

Properties Inspector

The Properties Inspector displays the attributes of the currently selected item on the page, whether it is an image, a piece of text, a table, a frame or an element of multimedia. In addition to viewing these attributes, they can also be altered by entering values within the Properties Inspector. For instance, if you want to change the size of an image, you can select it and then enter the new size that is required. To display the properties of a certain element it has to be selected first.

When using images on a website, create a separate folder in which to store them. This way you will always know where the source for your images is.

Image properties

Select an image by clicking on it once to display its relevant Properties Inspector:

Size   Dimensions   Location   Alt tag

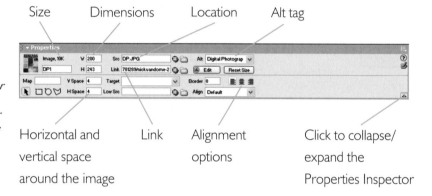

The collapse or expand option is available for the Properties Inspector regardless of the item selected.

Horizontal and vertical space around the image

Link

Alignment options

Click to collapse/ expand the Properties Inspector

Text properties

Select a paragraph of text by inserting the cursor anywhere within it, or select specific pieces of text by clicking and dragging the cursor over them:

Style   Font   Type size   Color   Bold/Italic

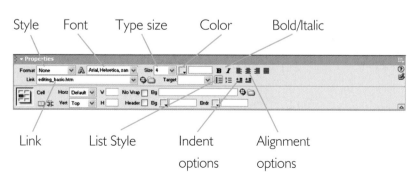

When you select a font in Dreamweaver the font box displays three alternatives for the most popular ones. This means that if the user does not have a particular font installed, the page will look for the next most suitable font, rather than automatically displaying the text in the system default font.

Link   List Style   Indent options   Alignment options

External editors

When designing Web pages, you will be working with a lot of elements that cannot be edited directly within Dreamweaver. The most obvious example of this is images, but it also applies to elements such as sound files or movie clips. One way to edit them would be to do so in an appropriate program before they are inserted into Dreamweaver. However, if you then need to edit the items again, once they have been imported, it can be frustrating having to open up the file again, edit it, and then re-import it. Dreamweaver simplifies this process by providing direct links to external programs that can be used to edit items while they are still in the Dreamweaver environment. This is know as using external editors.

The most commonly used external editors with Dreamweaver are for editing HTML code and editing images. HTML editing can be done with a text editor (such as Notepad on a PC or SimpleText on a Mac) and images can be edited with a graphics program such as Fireworks or Photoshop. Dreamweaver integrates very closely with Fireworks and so this is the best option when working with images, if possible.

It is possible to specify which program you want to use for specific tasks e.g. editing images, by selecting the file type and the program from the File Types/Editors category of the Preferences window:

1 Select Edit>Preferences from the Menu bar

2 Click here to select a file type

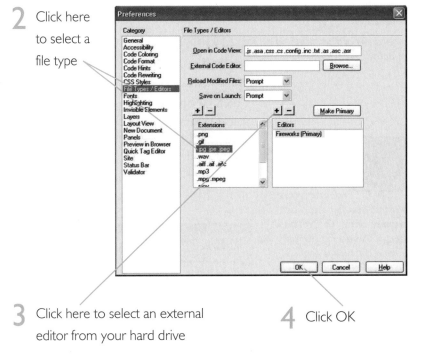

3 Click here to select an external editor from your hard drive

4 Click OK

Using external editors

Once you have selected the required external editors for different file formats, it is then possible to access them while you are working on a page:

1 Select an element on a page, such as an image

2 Right-click (Windows) Ctrl+click (Mac) on the item and select the Edit With option that contains the primary editor for the selected item. To edit the item with a different editor, select Edit With and then browse to the program that you want to use to edit the selected item

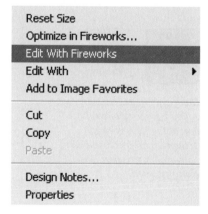

3 To change the external editor for a specific file type at any time, select Edit>Edit with External Editor, from the Menu bar and change the selection in the File Types/Editors dialog box, as shown on the facing page

Page properties

In addition to setting preferences that affect all of the files you work on in Dreamweaver, it is also possible to set properties for individual pages. This includes items such as background color, the color of links and the margins on the page. To set page properties:

If you are using a background image on a Web page, make sure it is not too complex or gaudy. This could create a dramatic initial effect, but if people are looking at the page a lot it could become irritating. Similarly, background colors should, in general, be subtle and unobtrusive, rather than bright and bold. White is a very effective background for Web pages.

Hyperlinks, or just links, can be colored differently depending on their current state. Different colors can be applied for a link before it has been activated, after it has been activated and when it is being pressed.

1   Select Modify>Page Properties from the Menu bar

2   Click here to select a background image for the active page, from your hard drive

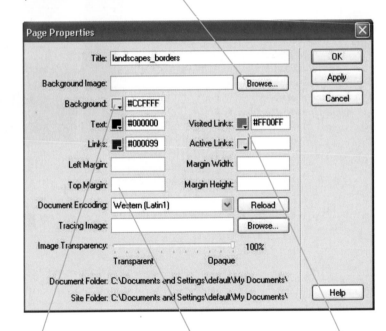

3   Click here to select a background color for the active page

5   In the Margin fields, set the margins for the active page

4   Click the Links fields to select a color for the links on the page

Page tabs and the toolbar

Page tabs

Almost invariably when a website is being created, a lot of different pages will be open at the same time. Keeping track of all of the open pages can be confusing, particularly if you are switching between different pages regularly. Dreamweaver MX has simplified this problem by displaying all of the open pages in the form of tabs at the bottom of each page. This means that, providing your monitor is large enough, all of the open documents can be viewed and accessed at any time:

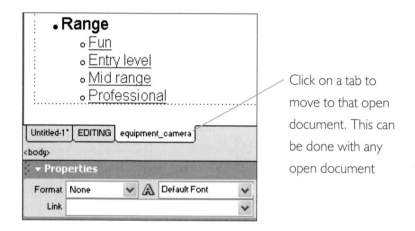

Click on a tab to move to that open document. This can be done with any open document

Toolbar

The Page Views options on the toolbar allow you to switch between the graphical layout or the HTML layout, or a combination of the two. For more information on this, see Chapter Three.

The toolbar at the top of the page has a number of options for specifying how Dreamweaver operates:

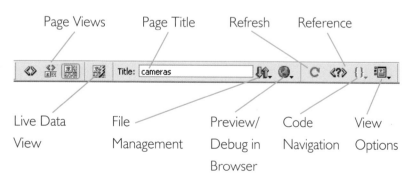

Page Views   Page Title   Refresh   Reference

Live Data View   File Management   Preview/ Debug in Browser   Code Navigation   View Options

Creating pages

When creating new pages, Dreamweaver MX offers considerably more flexibility than a blank page (with no formatting or pre-inserted elements) when File>New is selected from the Menu bar. Although this can certainly be done (by selecting Basic Page under the General tab) there is a lot more versatility when creating documents from scratch:

1 Select File>New from the Menu bar

2 Click on the General tab

3 Select the type of document you want to create

4 Click Create

5 A new document is opened and its type is displayed in the address bar

Page Design templates

One of the options when creating new pages is to use one of the page designs that have already been stored within Dreamweaver MX. This can be a good way to quickly create the basis of professionally designed Web pages. To use page design templates:

1 Select File>New from the Menu bar

2 Click on the General tab

Once a document has been created based on a page design the content can be customized to meet your own requirements. Restricted level or Guest users cannot install applications.

3 Select Page Designs and the design you want to use

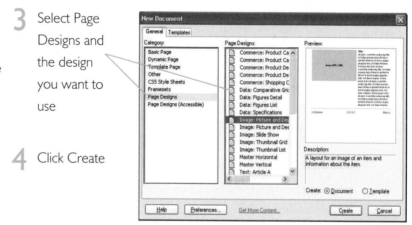

4 Click Create

5 A new document is created, based on the page design selected above:

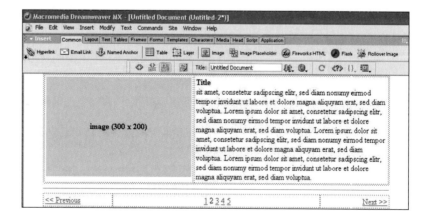

Accessibility

Accessibility options

An increasingly important issue for websites and Web designers is the one of accessibility. This concerns the use of the Web by blind or partially-sited users. Despite the visual nature of the Web, this group of users can still access the information by using a technology that reads the content on screen. This means that someone who is blind or partially-sighted is provided with an audio version of websites, rather than just a visual one.

The accessibility guidelines used by Dreamweaver MX are based on those contained in Section 508 of the 1998 Rehabilitation Act.

Dreamweaver MX enables you to add accessibility features to Web pages as they are being created. To do this:

1 Select Edit>Preferences from the Menu bar and click Accessibility

2 Check on the items that you want to have accessibility features applied to

Two websites to look at for more information about accessibility issues are the Section 508 site at www.section508.gov *and the Web Accessibility Initiative (WAI) at* www.w3.org/wai.

3 Click OK

4 Whenever one of the elements checked above is added to a Web page, a dialog box appears in which you can add the appropriate accessibility features:

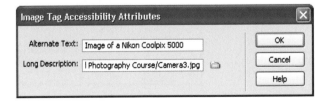

...cont'd

Checking accessibility

In addition to adding accessibility features to elements of a Web page, Dreamweaver MX also provides a function for checking a site to see if it meets standard accessibility guidelines. To check a site for accessibility compliance:

1 Select File>Check Page>Check Accessibility from the Menu bar

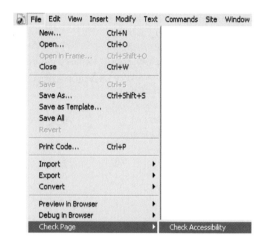

In an accessibility report, an item with a red cross next to it is one that breaches some aspect of the accessibility guidelines; an item with a question mark next to it is one that could cause some confusion for an accessibility reader when it is trying to interpret the page.

2 An accessibility report is generated automatically, with a description for each item

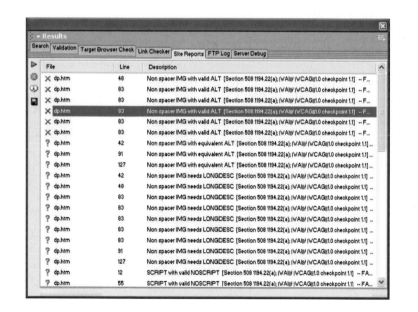

One website that can give reports on the accessibility of a site is Bobby at `http://bobby.watchfire.com/bobby.`

Getting help

The Help menu also has an option for registering your copy of Dreamweaver. This is done online by connecting to the Macromedia website and once you have gone through the registration process you will be able to get technical support for the product and also receive the latest information about updates and upgrades.

In common with most software programs, Dreamweaver offers an extensive range of Help items. These include a general Help index, online demonstrations of using the program and websites for the latest upgrades.

Dreamweaver Help

The main Help index is displayed in a browser window. This has a variety of options, all of which are accessed from the Help button on the Menu bar. The Answers panel also provides access to a variety of Help topics, including the latest updates from the Macromedia website.

Access Help topics here

Click here to access online updates

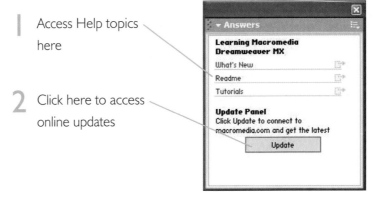

The Dreamweaver MX Help files can be accessed by pressing F12 on the keyboard.

Reference panel

The Reference panel is a Help feature provided by the respected publishers O'Reilly. It provides detailed information about the selected item on the page:

Click here to access the Reference panel

Click here to access additional reference categories

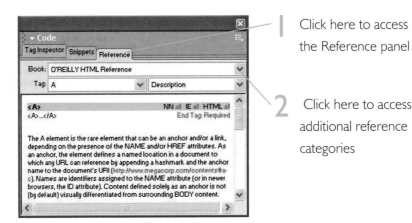

Setting up a site

Before you start creating Web pages it is important to set up a site structure into which all of your page content will be placed. This chapter looks at setting up a site and defining the elements within it.

Covers

Chapter Two

Planning a site

Websites that are published on the Internet are not just random pages that are thrown together in the hope that people will be able to view them over the Web. Instead, each site is a group of pages, images and, if applicable, multimedia effects, that are linked together by a structure that is invariably created before any of the pages are created. It is possible to create Web pages outside a Web structure in Dreamweaver and store them on your own computer. However, when it comes to creating a whole site it is important that you create a structure into which you can place all of the content for your site. When it comes to publishing your website on the Internet, you would encounter numerous problems if you had not already set up a site structure.

Do not create a new site in an existing folder that has other files in it. If you do, Dreamweaver will include all of these files in your site structure, even if they are not appropriate.

Preparing a structure

Before you start working with the site structure tools in Dreamweaver, it is a good idea to decide where you want to store your sites on your own hard drive. The pages and other content for a website are stored in a folder on your hard drive in exactly the same way as any other file. It is therefore a good idea to create a new folder for all of your Web authoring files. As you create sites, you can create sub-folders from the main folder for each new site. Also, for each site you may want to create sub-folders for all of the images and so on in your site. If you do this before you start creating your Web pages, it will make it easier to save and add pages to a site. Once you have set up your folder structure it could look something like this:

Draw a rough sketch of your proposed site structure before you start creating folders and files. This does not have to be the definitive structure, but it will give you a good overview of what you are trying to achieve.

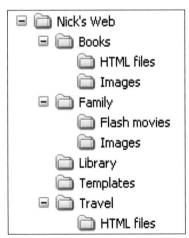

Creating a new site

After you have created a folder structure for your websites, you can begin to create individual sites within Dreamweaver. Once a site has been created, the content can then be added and built upon. If all of the items are stored within the same site structure you will be able to perform a variety of site management tasks with Dreamweaver. Within Dreamweaver MX there are options for a Basic and Advanced method of setting up sites. Both of them arrive at the same end result, but the Basic method guides you through the process with a wizard.

Basic site definition

You can create as many different structures for different websites as you like. But make sure each one has its own root folder.

1 Select Site>New Site from the Menu bar

2 Click the Basic tab

3 Enter a name for the site. Click Next

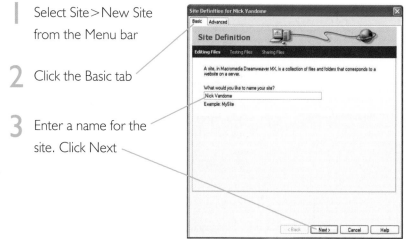

Try and give your sites easily identifiable names, rather than just My Site or Website. If you are going to be creating a lot of websites, this is particularly important so that you can quickly identify which is which.

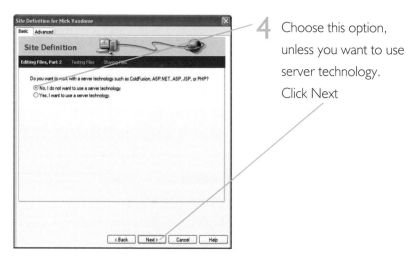

4 Choose this option, unless you want to use server technology. Click Next

5 Choose this option to edit your files on your own computer before they are published

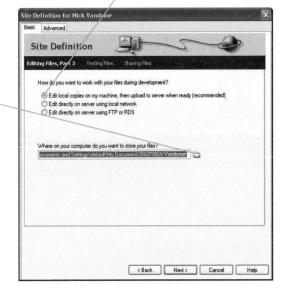

6 Click here to browse to a folder for storing your local files. Click Next

7 Click here to select the location of the remote server i.e. where your files are going to be published to. Select Local/ Network to experiment by publishing them on your own computer. Select FTP to publish them to a remote server. Click Next

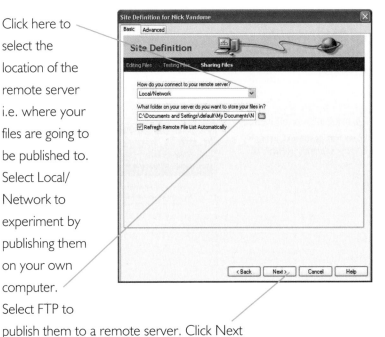

For more information on publishing via FTP see Chapter Eleven.

8 Choose this option (unless you are working in a shared environment i.e. one in which several people are editing the files within a single site). Click Next

Checking files in and out is used when a team is working on a website and it is necessary to be aware of which files are being edited at any one time. For more information on this, see Chapter Eleven.

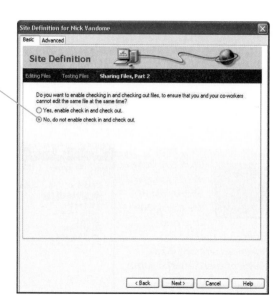

9 The final page gives a summary of the selections you have made. Click on Done to close the Site Definition window or Back to change the details

Advanced site definition

1 Select Site>New Site
from the Menu bar and
click the Advanced tab

2 Enter the
name for the
new site

*Click any item
in the column
on the left of
the dialog box
to access
additional options for
Advanced site definition.
Some of these are the same
as for the Basic site
definition wizard and the
information is entered in a
window similar to the one
for the advanced Local Info.*

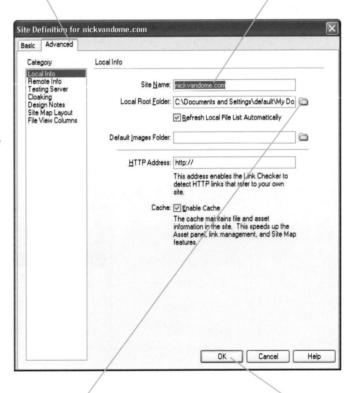

3 Click here to browse your hard drive
for the folder in which the new site
will be stored. This is known as the
root folder for the site

4 Click
OK

Setting up a home page

Every website has to have a home page. This is the one that appears when the site is first accessed and as far as the browser viewing the site is concerned, everything within the site is created relative to the home page. This can be particularly important when you are performing certain site management tasks, because Dreamweaver needs to know what is the home page, to use this as a reference point. There are two ways to define a home page in Dreamweaver.

Name the home page in each Dreamweaver site, "index.htm" or "index.html". They can be given other names, but these are the ones that work most effectively within Dreamweaver.

From the Site Definition window

The home page can be specified in the Site Definition window when a site is first defined or it can be edited once the site has been created. Either way, the process for specifying the home page is the same:

The Site Definition window can be accessed from either Design view or the Site panel. For both, select Site>New Site from the Menu bar to create a new site. To edit an existing site, select Site>Edit Sites from the Menu bar, select the site you want to edit and select Edit.

1 Select Site Map Layout in the Site Definition window

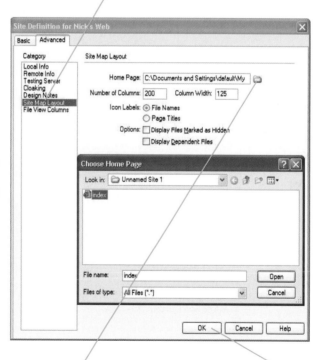

2 Click here to browse for a home page in the Choose Home Page dialog box. Select a file and click Open

3 Click OK

From the Site panel

Click on the Site panel
and select a file from
the local directory

Get into the
habit of naming
a home page at
the same time
as any new
sites are created.

You can also set
the home page
by right-clicking
(Windows) or
Ctrl+clicking
(Mac) on a file in the Site
panel and selecting Set as
Home Page from the
contextual menu.

2 Click Site

New Site...	
Edit Sites...	
Connect	Ctrl+Alt+Shift+F5
Get	Ctrl+Shift+D
Check Out	Ctrl+Alt+Shift+D
Put	Ctrl+Shift+U
Check In	Ctrl+Alt+Shift+U
Undo Check Out	
Cloaking	▶
Reports...	
Check Links Sitewide	Ctrl+F8
Change Link Sitewide...	
Synchronize...	
Recreate Site Cache	
Remove Connection Scripts	
Link to New File...	Ctrl+Shift+N
Link to Existing File...	Ctrl+Shift+K
Change Link...	Ctrl+L
Remove Link	Ctrl+Shift+L
Open Source of Link	
New Home Page...	
Set as Home Page	

3 Select Set as Home
Page from the Site
menu

Viewing the site map

The site map is a website management tool that displays a graphical representation of all of the files in the current site and the way that they relate to each other. Each file in the site map is defined in relation to the home page. This is one reason why it is important to specify a home page. The site map shows the links between various files within the current site and also any files that have broken links. To access the site map:

To return to File view, select Local View from the drop-down menu in the Site panel.

Select Site>Site Map or click here in the Site panel and select Map View

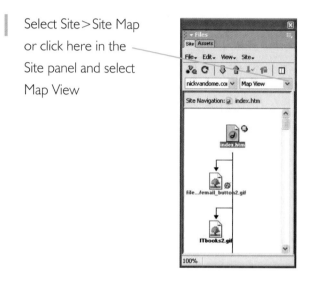

New files and folders can be added to a site by clicking on the File menu in the Site panel and selecting New File or New Folder. However, this does not offer as much versatility as creating new files from the main Menu bar.

3 Click here to view the site map and the local files

2 Click here to expand and collapse the Site panel

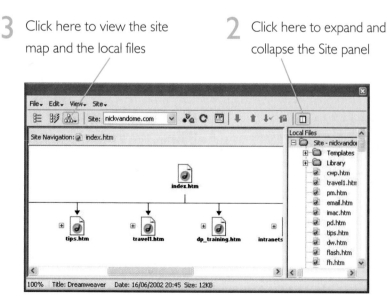

Defining a site

A site can be defined when it is first created and it is also possible to change these settings once a site has been set up. To create or edit the definition of a site:

1 Click here in the Site panel and select Edit Sites

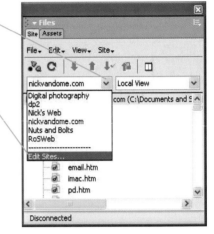

Other categories in the Site Definition box include:
Remote Info which covers aspects of publishing a site and is looked at in more detail in Chapter Eleven; Testing Server which is used with dynamic Web pages, and is looked at in more detail in Chapter Ten; and Cloaking which can be used to prevent certain files being published, and is looked at in more detail in Chapter Eleven.

2 Select a site and click on Edit

Design Notes is a function that allows designers to add notes to Web pages as they are working on them. This can be particularly useful if a team of designers are working on the same site.

3 Click here to select the options for using Design Notes within a site

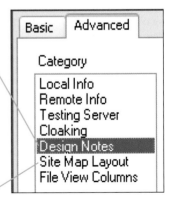

4 Click here to select options affecting the layout of the Site Map

HTML in Dreamweaver

This chapter looks at the options that Dreamweaver provides for adding and editing HTML (HyperText Markup Language) code, which is used to create Web pages. It shows how to create your own code and covers some of the features that assist in the process, such as the Tag Chooser and code snippets.

Covers

Chapter Three

HTML overview

HyperText Markup Language (HTML) is the computer code used to create Web pages. It is not a fully-blown computer programming language, but rather a set of instructions that enables a Web browser to determine the layout of pages.

HTML is created by using a series of tags, which contain the instructions that are interpreted by the browsers. These tags are placed around the item to which you want that particular command to apply. Most tags, but not all of them, have an opening and a closing element. The opening tag contains the particular command and the closing tag contains the same command, but with a / in front of it, to denote the end of the command. For instance, if you wanted to display a piece of text as bold, you could do it with the following piece of HTML:

For more detailed information about HTML, take a look at "HTML in easy steps".

This text would appear bold in a browser

HTML is a text-based code which means that the source HTML file only contains text and not any images or multimedia items. These appear in the browser because of a reference to them that is placed in a HTML document. For instance, if you wanted to include an image in a document you would insert the following piece of HTML into your source file:

<img src="myimage.jpg">

This would instruct the browser to insert this image at the required point within the HTML document when it is being viewed on the Web. It is possible to insert HTML code to instruct a variety of graphics and multimedia files to be displayed in a Web page. However, it is important to remember that when you are publishing your pages, all of the items that are referred to in the source HTML document are uploaded to the server as well as the HTML file.

Since Dreamweaver is a What You See Is What You Get (WYSIWYG) program, it generates all of the HTML in the background. This means that it is possible to ignore its existence completely. However, it is useful to learn the basics.

Underlined text should only be used as a design feature on Web pages in exceptional circumstances. This is because hyperlinks (the device used to move to other pages and websites) usually appear underlined to denote their status. If normal text is also underlined, this could cause confusion.

For more information about images on Web pages, see Chapter Six.

Tables are an excellent way to format a variety of different content on a Web page. They do not just have to be used for formatting words or figures. For more information about tables, see Chapter Eight.

Common tags

Unless otherwise stated, tags use the equivalent closing tag by inserting / in front of the command. Some of the most commonly used tags in HTML are:

- `<p>` This creates a new paragraph

- `<b>` This creates bold text

- `<i>` This creates italics

- `<u>` This creates underlined text

- `<br>` This inserts a line break (this does not have a closing tag)

- `<hr>` This inserts a horizontal line (this does not have a closing tag)

- `<img src="image.jpg">` This inserts the specified image

- `<font face="Arial">` This specifies a certain font. The closing tag is just `</font>`

- `<h1>` This formats text at a preset heading size. There are six levels for this: h1 being the largest and h6 being the smallest. Paragraph and other formatting tags cannot be used within heading tags

- `<table>` This inserts a table

- `<color="ffffff">` This can be used to select a color for a variety of items, including background color and text color

- `<a href="default.htm">Home Page</a>` This is used to create a hyperlink to another Web page. In this case the link is to the file 'default.htm' and the words 'Home Page' will appear underlined on the Web page, denoting that it is a link to another page

Page views

Although it is possible to be blissfully unaware of the existence of HTML when you are using Dreamweaver, you can also hand-code pages using Code view or the HomeSite/Code-Styler workspace. This allows you to create your own HTML code, which is then translated into the document window by Dreamweaver. This can be a good way to learn about HTML and perform fine-tuning tasks if you cannot achieve it through the document window. In Dreamweaver MX you can access the graphical version of the page, the HTML code on its own or a combination of them both:

Click here to access Code and Design view together

Click here to access Design view on its own

 When Code view and Design view are showing together, if any changes are made to one of these views, the other is updated automatically.

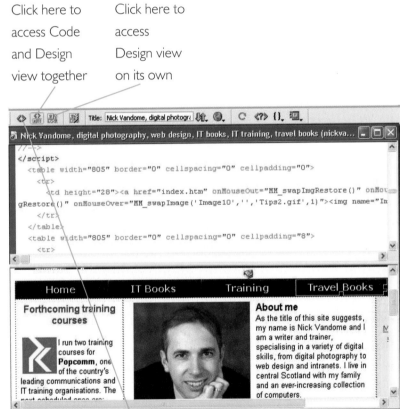

Click here to access the Code view on its own

HTML preferences

Code colors

When creating and editing HTML within Dreamweaver, it is possible to set various defaults for the colors within the HTML Source window. This can not only be useful for aesthetic reasons, but also to make specific elements stand out within the code. These elements can then be quickly identified when working with the source code. To set the preferences for colors within the Code Source window:

Use a consistent theme for colors within the HTML Source window, so that you can easily recognize different elements within the code even if you are working on different websites.

1 Select Edit>Preferences from the Menu bar

2 Select Code Coloring in the Preferences dialog box

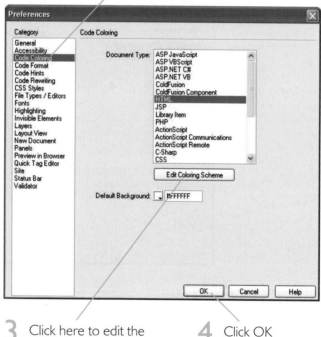

As with all of the color palettes within Dreamweaver, it is possible to apply a wider range of colors for the HTML options than the ones on the standard palette that appears. Click on the paint palette at the bottom right-corner to create your own custom colors.

3 Click here to edit the existing color scheme

4 Click OK

The options for setting colors for Code Coloring are:

- Background. This affects the background color of the window

- Text. This affects the color of the text that appears in the document

- Bold, Italic and Underlining

1 Select a tag from this list

2 Click here to select a font color

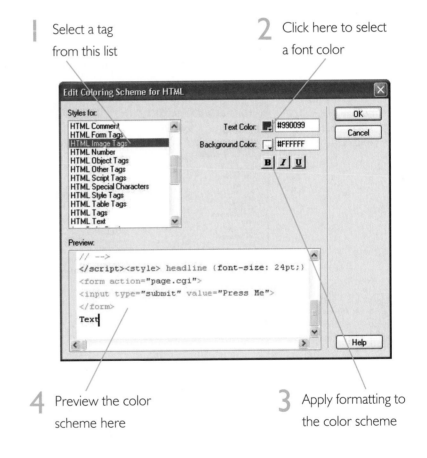

4 Preview the color scheme here

3 Apply formatting to the color scheme

Code format

These preferences can be used to determine the layout of the code within the HTML Source window. These include the format for how tags are presented and also the use of indents and tabs to indicate certain elements, such as tables and frames. To access the Code Format preferences:

According to the values that are set, different elements on a page will be displayed with code that is indented in the HTML Source. For instance, the code for table rows and columns and frames is usually indented.

Select Code Format from the Preferences dialog box

Click here to specify how indents are displayed and which items will appear indented

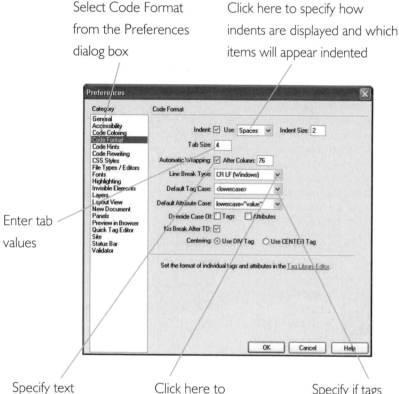

Enter tab values

Before you start creating Web pages, decide whether you want your tags to be in upper or lower case. Once you have done this, stick to it for all of your pages and sites, for the sake of consistency. In general, lowercase tags are neater and take up less room.

Specify text wrapping i.e. how many characters before the text is moved to the next line

Click here to determine how different servers on the Web deal with line breaks within your source code

Specify if tags and attributes are displayed in upper or lower case

Tag Chooser

To speed up the process of creating HTML, Dreamweaver has a number of functions for inserting HTML tags or blocks of code, rather than having to create it all by hand. One of these is the Tag Chooser where HTML tags can be inserted with a couple of mouse clicks. To do this:

Once the Insert button is clicked in the Tag Chooser dialog box the selected tag is entered into Code view but the dialog box remains visible until Close is clicked. Therefore keep the Code view window visible so that you can see when the code has been added. This means that you can add several tags without having to activate the Tag Chooser dialog box each time.

1 Insert the cursor in Code View, at the point where you want the tag to appear

2 Right-click (Windows) or Ctrl+click (Mac) and select Insert Tag

3 In the Tag Chooser window select the tag you want to use and click Insert

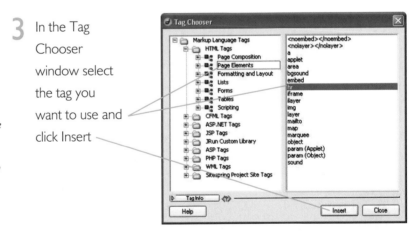

Some tags have additional properties that can be added in a dialog box once the tag has been selected.

4 The tag is inserted into the document at the insertion point

Tag Libraries

The tags that appear in the Tag Chooser are stored in the Tag Library. It is possible to add tags to the Tag Library and also edit existing ones. This gives increased versatility for the HTML tags at your disposal. To edit tags in the Tag Library:

1 Select Edit>Tag Libraries from the Menu bar

2 Select a tag to view its attributes and edit them as required

3 Click here to create a new library for your own tags or to create new tags. Click OK

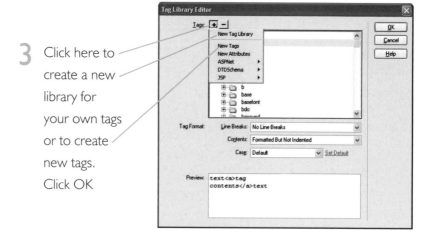

You may want to create new Tag Libraries and tags if you are using a server technology such as Active Server Pages or ColdFusion.

4 For a new Tag Library, enter a name and click OK

Tag Inspector

The Tag Inspector is a panel that enables you to see the attributes for a selected item, and amend them if required. To use the Tag Inspector:

1 Select an item to view its properties in the Tag Inspector

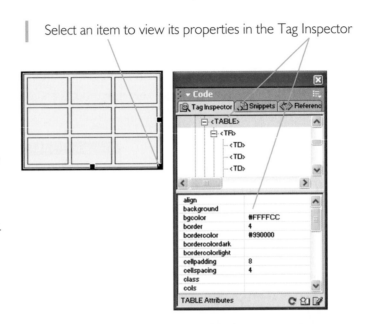

Depending on the item selected, the attributes shown in the Tag Inspector will be fewer for some items than for others.

2 Select an attribute and enter details here to change its parameters

3 Click here to Refresh the Tag Inspector, if several changes have been made to the items within it

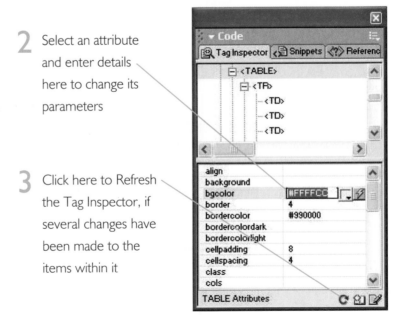

4 The changes in the Tag Inspector will be made to the selected object

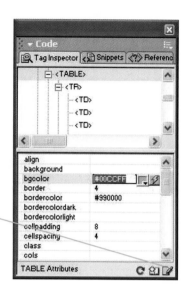

5 Click here to access the Tag Editor for the selected tag

Once a change has been made to a tag in the Tag Editor, this only applies to the selected item. It does not apply to any similar items that are subsequently created.

6 Enter new parameters for the tag in the Tag Editor

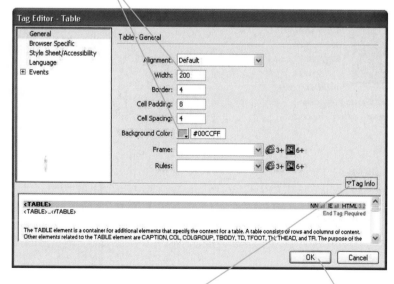

7 Click here to view reference information about the selected tag

8 Click OK

Code snippets

One of the new features of Dreamweaver MX is the ability to add blocks, or snippets, of HTML code into documents. This is done with the Snippets panel and existing snippets can be used as well as creating new ones. To use the Snippets panel:

Code snippets are grouped in folders containing similar types of snippets. However, it is possible to move snippets and also folders by dragging and dropping them to another folder.

1 Click the Snippets panel tab to view the current Snippets folders

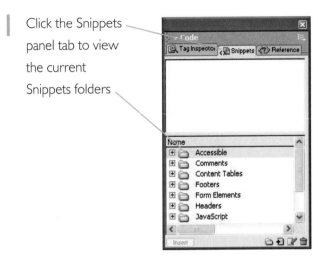

Even though their name suggests otherwise, code snippets can include some lengthy elements of HTML code.

2 Select a folder by double-clicking on it and select a snippet within it by clicking on it once

3 Click Insert

Metadata is contained within the <head> tag of a HTML page and it is used to store items such as keywords and descriptions about a page, which can be used by search engines trying to locate the page. Metadata can also include items such as information about how frequently a page should be automatically refreshed by the browser.

A lot of snippets that follow accessibility guidelines can be found in the Accessible folder.

4 The selected snippet of code is inserted into the current document. Depending on the type of snippet, it will be displayed in Design view and Code view. However, some snippets, such as meta information, will only be displayed in Code view

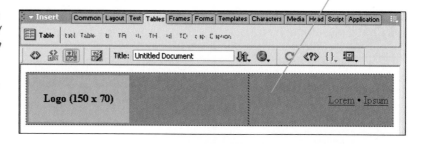

5 To edit an existing snippet, select it in the Snippets panel and click here

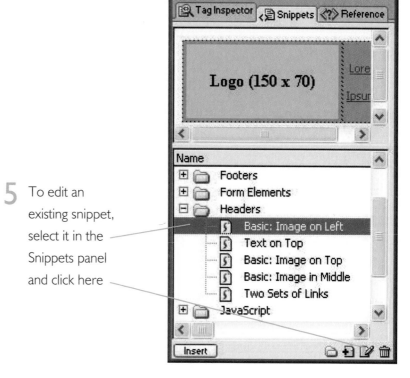

6 The code that makes up the snippet is displayed in the Snippet dialog box

Two very useful snippets can be found in the Navigation folder in the Snippets panel. They are in the Breadcrumb sub-folder and they can be used at the top of a page to denote where exactly within a site the user has reached.

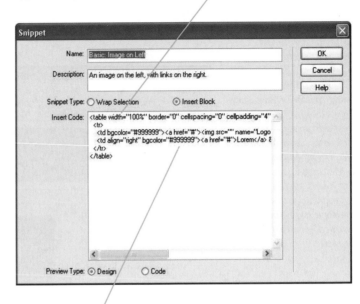

7 Make any changes that are required and click OK

Any piece of code that you think you will want to use frequently should be saved as a snippet.

Creating new snippets

Click here in the Snippets panel to create a new snippet folder

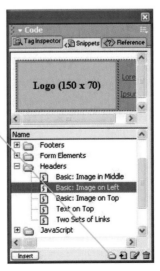

2 Enter a name for the new snippets folder

The HTML code for inserting an image can be created as a snippet in the same way as any other piece of HTML code i.e. select the image and select New Snippet from the Snippets panel menu.

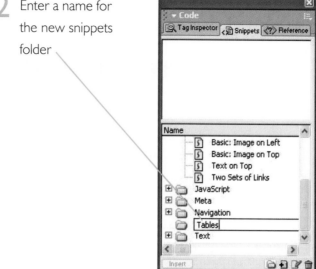

3 Select an object or a piece of HTML code

4 Click here to select the Snippets panel menu and select New Snippet

5 The code for the snippet is already inserted. Enter a name and description for the snippet and, if necessary, amend the code

The Preview Type can be set to Design or Code. This determines how the snippet is displayed in the Preview panel of the Snippets panel. Design gives a graphical preview and Code displays the HTML.

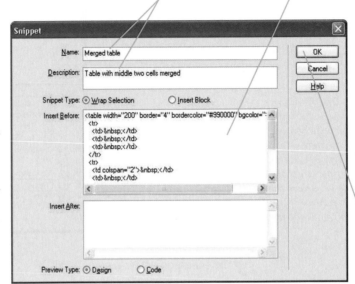

6 Click OK

7 The new snippet is added to the new folder in the Snippets panel and can now be used in the same way as any other snippet

Roundtrip HTML

A file has to be saved and placed within a site structure before an external editor can be used to edit the HTML code.

With the inclusion of the HomeSite HTML editor within Dreamweaver, the need for using an external HTML editor has been reduced considerably (Windows only). For the Mac, the BBEdit editor can be used as a powerful external editor.

To select an external editor for HTML files, select Edit> Preferences from the Menu bar and select the File Types/Editors category. Then click the Browse button next to the External Code Editor box and select an editor from your hard drive.

Roundtrip HTML is a feature unique to Dreamweaver that allows you to edit your source code in an external text editor and then automatically update the changes in the Dreamweaver document. It is even possible to set a variety of preferences so that Dreamweaver will correct any coding or syntax errors that have occurred while you have been editing the document in an external editor. This can be useful if you are used to working with a text editor, such as Notepad on a PC or SimpleText on a Mac. In addition to using these types of editor for HTML coding it is also possible to use them for more complicated programming such as Javascript and VB Script, if you are so inclined. To use Roundtrip HTML:

1 Open a document and select Edit>Edit with External Editor from the Menu bar

2 Edit the code in the external HTML editor and save the file

3 In Dreamweaver a dialog box will inform you that the file has been modified outside Dreamweaver. Click Yes to accept the changes

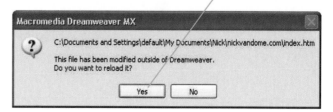

Invalid code

If you write any invalid code in the Code view, or turn off all of the HTML Rewriting preferences when opening a document from another source, any invalid code will be highlighted in yellow, in both the Code view window and the Design view window. This means that Dreamweaver has encountered some code that it does not understand and therefore it cannot display it correctly or reformat it automatically. However, it is possible to manually correct any invalid code:

On occasions, a whole string of HTML tags will be marked as being invalid. However, this can sometimes be corrected by fixing one tag, such as changing its nesting order.

1 Click on the tags that denote invalid HTML code. This can be done in either the Code view window or Design view

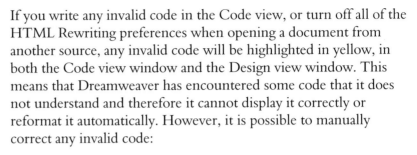

If you are familiar with HTML, it can be quicker to fix invalid code in the Code view window rather than Design view.

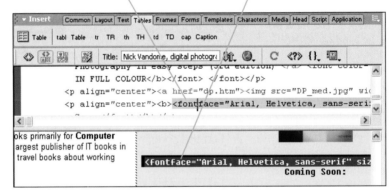

2 A window will appear alerting you to the reasons for the invalid code and instructing you how to repair it. Follow these instructions and check that the invalid code tags have subsequently disappeared

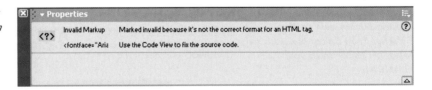

If you encounter any invalid code on your pages, press F12 to see how this affects the page when it is viewed in a browser. In some cases it will be unnoticeable.

Cleaning up HTML

One of the problems with WYSIWYG Web authoring programs is that they tend to create a certain amount of superfluous or redundant HTML coding. Although Dreamweaver is more efficient in this respect than a lot of similar programs, it does still produce some unnecessary code. This results in files not being as 'clean' as possible. This does not necessarily have an effect on the way a Web page looks, but it can create larger file sizes. Generally the more complex that a design is, then the more unnecessary HTML code will be created.

Dreamweaver has a facility for checking the source HTML code in documents, to ensure that it is as clean as possible. To do this:

If you can make your HTML code as clean as possible, you may gain greater respect from any HTML experts who look at your source code when your pages are on the Web.

1 Open a page in the document window and select Commands> Clean Up HTML (or Clean Up Word HTML) from the Menu bar

HTML documents can be created in Microsoft Word and then opened in Dreamweaver. However, they are notorious for creating a lot of unnecessary code, which is why there is an option for cleaning up HTML created in Word.

2 Check on the boxes for the clean up functions that you want to apply. Click OK to apply them

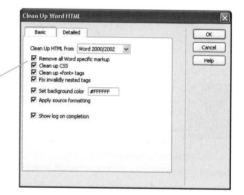

3 A dialog box will appear informing you of the clean up operations that have been performed. Click OK

Quick Tag editor

When editing HTML code there will probably be times when you want to quickly change or add a specific tag. This can be done by accessing Code view. However, it is also possible to do this without leaving Design view, through the use of the Quick Tag editor. This is a function that enables you to insert and check HTML tags directly in the Design view window. Any changes that are made are updated automatically in the Code view window. The Quick Tag editor can be accessed by selecting Modify>Quick Tag Editor from the Menu bar or by using Ctrl+T (Windows) or Command+T (Mac). This shortcut can also be used to toggle between the different modes of the Quick Tag editor.

There are two different modes that can be used within the Quick Tag editor:

When inserting tags with the Quick Tag editor it is best to also insert the corresponding closing tag at the required point. Check in the HTML Source window to make sure that the tags have been inserted in the correct places.

Insert HTML mode

This enables you to insert new HTML tags into a document. If required, it can be used to insert a string of several tags together. If the closing tags are not inserted, then Dreamweaver will place these automatically in the most appropriate place.

Insert HTML mode can be used to insert both opening and closing tags and also the content between them.

| Insert the cursor at the point where you want to create a new HTML tag. Do not select any elements on the page

Forthcoming training courses

Once tags have been entered in the Quick Tag Editor the changes can be applied by clicking back in Design view.

2   Select Ctrl+T (Windows) or Command +T (Mac) and enter the required tag and any content. If you wait a couple of seconds a drop-down hints menu will appear with a choice of tags to use

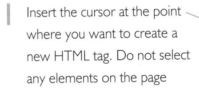

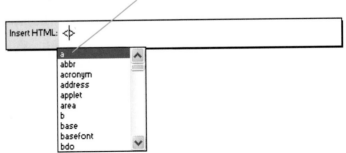

Edit Tag mode

This can be used to edit existing HTML tags in a document. The Quick Tag editor opens in this mode if an item with an opening and closing tag is selected on the page:

The Quick Tag editor can also be accessed by clicking on this icon on the Properties Inspector:

1 Select an element on the page that contains an opening tag, content and a closing tag. This could include selecting an image, or an entire piece of formatted text

2 Select Ctrl+T (Windows) or Command +T (Mac) to open the Quick Tag editor in Edit Tag mode

In Edit Tag mode, you can edit tags manually i.e. write the HTML tags yourself, or insert a new tag from the hints menu that appears after a couple of seconds.

```
Edit Tag: <img src="Nick4.jpg" width="200"
          height="219" align="left" hspace="10"
          alt="Nick Vandome">
```

3 Edit the tag and then apply the changes by clicking back in the Design view window

```
Edit Tag: <img src="Nick4.jpg" width="400"
          height="438" align="left" hspace="10"
          alt="Nick Vandome">
```

4 If you enter an incorrect tag, you will be alerted to this by a warning dialog box

Selecting and removing tags

Selecting tags

In addition to selecting tags with the Quick Tag Editor by selecting items in the document window it is also possible to select them from the tag selector which is located at the bottom left of the document window. This enables you to easily identify the opening and closing tags and also the content which is contained within them. To select tags using the tag selector:

Some tags appear in the tag selector when items are selected by clicking on them in the document window. Others, such as the body tag, are visible all of the time.

The relevant tags are displayed in the tag selector, which is located at the bottom left of the document window

The tags displayed in the tag selector can also be used to access the Quick Tag Edit mode. To do this, right-click (Windows) or Ctrl+click (Mac) on the required tag in the tag selector – the Quick Tag editor will open in Edit mode, using the highlighted tag.

2 Select a tag by clicking on it once. The equivalent item is highlighted in the document window. This can then be edited using the Quick Tag editor

Removing tags

Right-click (Windows) or Ctrl+click (Mac) on one of the tags in the tag selector and select Remove Tag from the contextual menu

Assets

The process of creating websites can involve using the same basic designs and elements several times over. This chapter explains how Dreamweaver allows the Web designer to use commonly used items across a website, through the use of the Assets panel. Two of the most powerful of these items are templates and the Library, which are looked at in detail in this chapter.

Covers

Chapter Four

Managing assets

The Assets panel is an area that keeps track of many of the elements that you use in creating your websites. This includes:

- Images

- Colors

- Hyperlinks

- Multimedia content such as Flash

- Video

- Scripts

- Templates

- Library items

The Assets panel will only show items for sites that have been defined. Once this has been done the Assets panel can recognize the items in the site's cache.

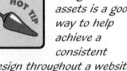

Using the color assets is a good way to help achieve a consistent design throughout a website. Colors can easily be used on multiple pages, without having to remember the exact one each time.

You do not have to add items to the Assets panel (except for templates and Library items) since all of the relevant content is automatically inserted into the Assets panel when it is inserted into the Dreamweaver page. There are two ways to manage Assets: either on a site-wide basis, or as Favorites, which are usually items that you want to use on several pages. To view the site assets:

The Assets panel can also be accessed by selecting Window>Assets from the Menu bar.

Click here to access the Assets panel

Select the Site button and click on the Refresh button to view the assets for the current site

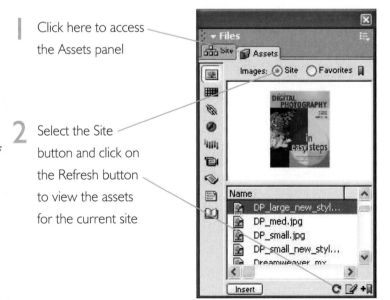

Creating Favorites

Assets that are going to be used regularly, such as an image that will appear on all the pages of a site, or a hyperlink back to the home page, can be added to the Favorites list for quick access. To do this:

The Favorites list can also be used to add new assets such as colors or hyperlinks.

Select an asset in the Site list and click here to add it to the Favorites

OR

To remove an asset from the Favorites list, select it in the Favorites panel and then click here:

Select an item in Design view and right-click (Windows) or Ctrl+click (Mac) and select the relevant Add To command

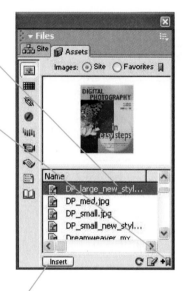

Applying assets

Assets are applied slightly differently depending on the item:

Assets can also be applied by dragging them from the Assets panel onto a page in Design view.

For images, Flash, Shockwave, video and scripts, select the item and then select Insert to place it on the page

For colors and links, select the relevant item in Design view, then select the asset and select Apply to have it take effect on the page

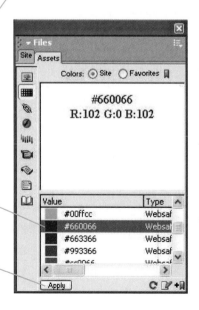

Using templates

Template files have been a common feature in word processing and Desktop Publishing programs for several years now. These are files that contain standard elements that recur in certain types of documents. The template can then be used to store the recurring items, and new content can also be added once a document is opened using the template as a foundation. This is an excellent device for producing a consistent design for items such as newsletters and brochures and it is also a timesaving device because the basic design only has to be created once.

When a new document is opened from a template the document is based on the template, rather than being the template file itself. When it is first opened, the document will display the same content as the template file, but new items can then be added.

Recognizing the value of templates for Web designers, Dreamweaver has powerful facilities for creating and using templates. This means that designers can quickly create a consistent theme for a website, while still retaining the freedom to add new content to pages.

Templates in Dreamweaver can be created from scratch or existing files can be converted into templates. New files can then be created, based on an existing template. It is also possible to edit the content of template files.

When templates are created you can specify which areas are constant e.g. a company logo, and which are editable. This gives you a good degree of control over the pages that are created from your templates.

The colors for the tags in templates can be changed by selecting Edit>Preferences from the Menu bar and then selecting Highlighting and a color for each of the regions within the template.

Some areas in a document created from a template remain static and cannot be edited, while others are fully editable. Editable regions are denoted by a blue tag, with the name of the region

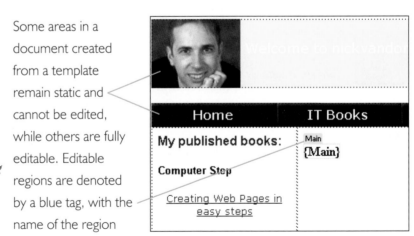

Creating templates

Templates can be created from scratch or existing files can be converted into templates.

Creating a new template

1 Click on the Make Template button on the Templates tab on the Insert panel

2 Enter the locked content for the template

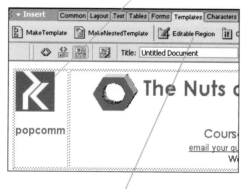

3 Click on the Editable Region button to create areas where content will be added to documents based on the template

4 Give the editable region a name and click OK

5 The editable region is highlighted in the template. This is the only
place where content can be added to any document based on
the template

6 Select File>Save As Template from the Menu bar and give the
template a name

*Saved
templates are
placed in a
Templates
folder within
the current site structure.
This folder is created
automatically by
Dreamweaver when a
template is first saved.*

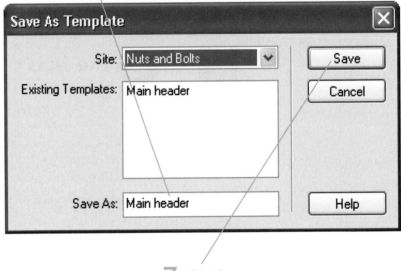

7 Click Save

Creating a template from an existing document

1   Open the document you want to use as a template:

2   Click on the Editable Region button on the Templates tab on the Insert Bar

3   Since editable regions can only be inserted into templates, a message will appear saying that the file will be converted into a template file. Click on OK

4 Enter a name for the new editable region

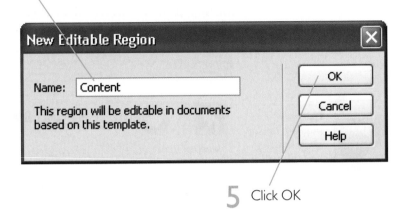

5 Click OK

When a file is saved as a template the original is also retained. This means that you can save as many files as you like from a template, safe in the knowledge that the original version will still be intact.

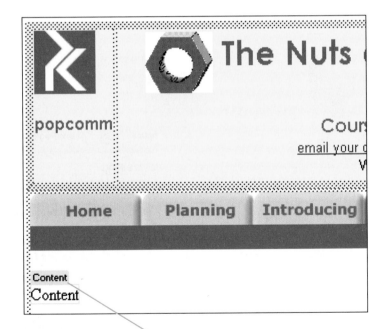

6 The document is now a template file with the required editable region inserted

7 Save the template as shown in Steps 6 and 7 on page 66

Editing templates

If you want to change the content of a particular template, this can be done by editing it. This changes the content for all of the documents that have been based on this template. So if you have ten documents based on a single template, the size of the headings in each one could be altered by editing the heading formatting in the template file. To edit a template:

Templates can also be edited by right-clicking (Windows) or Ctrl+clicking (Mac) in a document based on a template and selecting Templates>Open Attached Template from the contextual menu.

If you are updating a template, check all of the files to which it is linked, to make sure that you want to make the intended editing change to all of them. If you do not, you can detach any of the files from the template by opening them and selecting Modify>Templates>Detach from Template from the Menu bar.

1 Access the Assets panel by clicking here

2 Click here to access the templates

3 Double-click on a template to open it

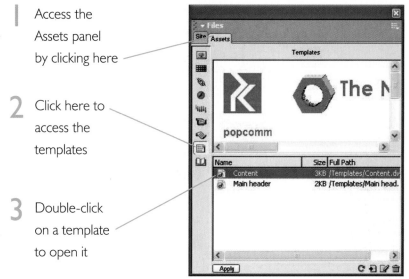

4 Edit the content of the template and select File>Save from the Menu bar

5 A dialog box will appear asking if you want to update all the documents based on this template. If you do, select Update

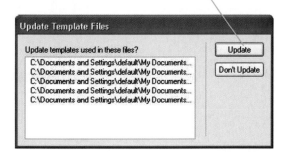

Repeating editable regions

In some cases it can be useful to create editable regions that can be repeated several times by the person creating documents based on the template. For instance, they may want to include table rows but are unsure how many they will want. If the row is created as a repeating editable region, they can add extra rows as they are needed. This also means that the basic structure of the template remains untouched, even though elements can be added to it. To create repeating editable regions:

Repeating editable regions are used in any documents based on the linked template rather than in the template itself. They are only created in the template but become active in the document.

1 Create a standard template and click on the Repeating Region button on the Insert panel's Templates tab

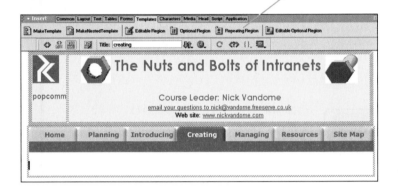

2 Create the elements that will be used as the repeating editable region. In this example, it is a table row

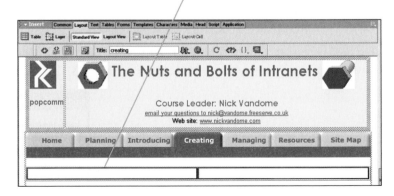

3 Insert the cursor where you want content to be added to the repeating editable region and click on the Editable Region button on the Templates tab on the Insert panel. Give the Editable Region a name and click OK

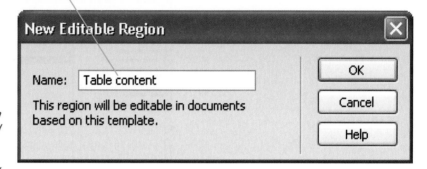

A repeating editable region on its own will not allow for content to be added. To do this, a normal editable region has to be included within the repeating editable region.

4 The editable region is added to the repeating region. This is where content will be added in each occurrence of the repeating region when content is added to a document based on this template

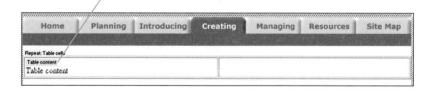

5 Save the template in the same way as shown on page 66

6   To use a template with a repeating editable region, select File>New from the Menu bar. Select the Templates tab and select the required template. Click Create

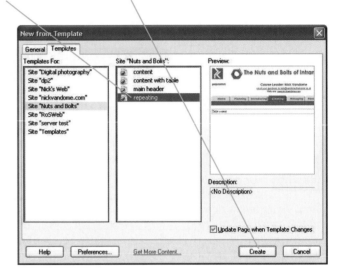

7   Enter content in the editable region

Use the Up and Down arrows at the top of the Repeating Editable Regions content box to move different regions up and down in the current order in which they appear.

8   Click here to add a repeating editable region, which can have its own content added

Template properties

Templates can have properties assigned to them in exactly the same way as standard pages. These properties are set in the Page Properties dialog box for the template. Once these properties are set they will apply to any documents that are created from the template and they will not be able to be altered in the document's page properties. The exception to this is the page title. To set a template's properties:

1 Open a template then select Modify>Page Properties from the Menu bar

2 Enter the properties that you want to apply to this template. These will also apply to any documents that are based on this template. When you are finished click OK

By setting the page properties for a template it is possible to change an element for several pages at once just by altering it in the template. For instance, if 20 pages are based on a template that has a background color set to blue, all of these pages can have their backgrounds changed to red simply by updating the background color in the template.

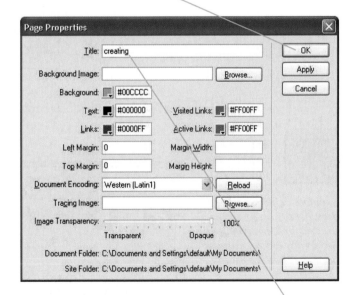

3 When a new document is created from the template, the only item that can be changed is the page Title. Any other changes that are made will not take effect

Creating pages from templates

Once templates have been created, it is then possible to produce new Web pages in Dreamweaver, based on these templates. To do this:

When templates are created, they are specific to the site in which they were produced. To use a template in another site, open it, select Save As Template from the Menu bar and then, in the Save As Template dialog box, select the site in which you want the template to be available.

1 Select File>New from the Menu bar and click on the Templates tab

2 Select a template that has already been created and click on Create

3 A new HTML document is opened, based on the selected template:

In a document based on a template, the outer border identifies the template on which the document is based and also the fact that everything within it is locked, unless it has been specified as an editable region.

4 The editable regions are displayed on the page and this is where content can be added

Nested templates

When you are working with templates there will probably be occasions when you will want to use the structure of one template but with slight amendments or additions. Rather than having to create two different templates, it is possible to use nested templates, when one template is based on an existing one. This has the advantage that the two templates can keep similar features, such as a logo or a navigation bar, while allowing their own unique content too. Also, any amendments to the original template are automatically recorded in any nested ones. To create nested templates:

1 Select a template in the Assets panel and click here to access the Assets menu

2 Select New from Template

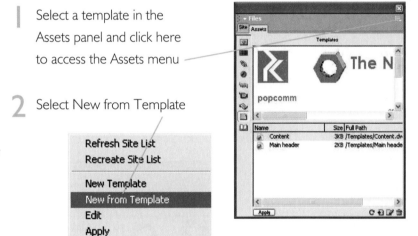

In addition to repeating editable regions and nested templates, the other new template option in Dreamweaver MX is the Optional Region function. This can be set to appear or be hidden in a document based on the linked template. This is done by entering coding in the New Optional Region dialog box once the Optional Region button has been clicked on the Template tab on the Insert panel. This requires some programming knowledge as it uses parameters and expressions.

3 A new document is opened. Click on the Make Nested Template button on the Insert panel's Templates tab

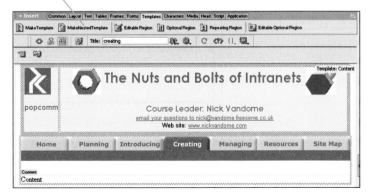

4 The document is then converted into a new template. Give it a
name in the Save As Template dialog box and click Save

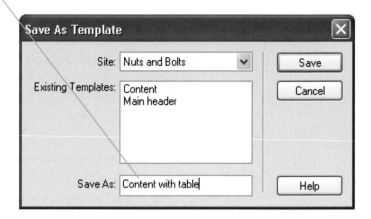

5 A new template is created, based on the original one. The content
from the original cannot be edited, but new content can be added

*The original
template must
have at least
one editable
region in order
for new content to be added
in the nested template.*

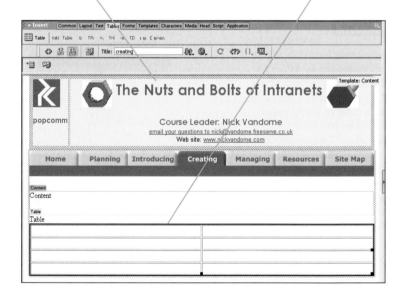

About the Library

During the design process of a website there will probably be some elements that you will want to reuse on different pages within the site. These could be static elements that appear on several pages, such as a company logo, or items where one part is updated regularly, such as a latest news section. Instead of having to create or insert these elements from their source location each time you want to use them, Dreamweaver has a facility for storing them and then dragging them onto a page whenever they are required. The location in which they are stored is known as the Library. Each site can have its own individual Library, with items that are used throughout that site.

Library items cannot be edited once they have been placed on a Web document page. Library items can be edited, but this has to be done through the Library panel.

When an item is placed in the Library it creates a Library item file that links to the source location in which that item is stored. So if the item is an image, there will be a link to its location on the hard drive. This means that the image can be reused numerous times without increasing the file size of the page. Rather than placing a copy of the item on a page each time it is taken from the Library, Dreamweaver creates a reference (or instance) back to the source location of the item. As long as the item is not moved from its source location then the Library version can be reused as many times as you like. Also, Library items can be updated, if required, and any changes made to them will be reflected in all of the instances of it in the site. To access the Library:

Before Library items can be created, the page from which they are being created has to be saved and placed within an existing site structure.

Click here on the Assets panel

Creating Library items

Items can be added to the Library from any open Dreamweaver document. These will then be available in the Library to all other pages within that site. To add items to the Library:

Blocks of text and images can be converted into Library items, as can tables and forms and more complicated elements such as Flash movies.

1 Open a file in Design view and make sure the Library panel is visible, as shown on the previous page

2 Select the item that you want to include in the Library

Images can be selected by clicking on them once and text can be selected by dragging the cursor over the required section.

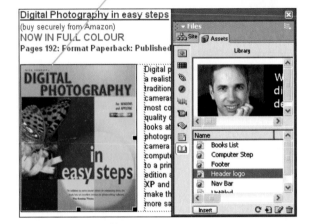

Items can also be added to the Library by selecting them and then selecting Modify>Library> Add Object to Library from the Menu bar, or clicking on the New Library Item button on the Assets panel.

3 Drag and drop the item into either panel of the Library

4 Type a name for the Library item

Adding items from the Library

Once items have been created in the Library, they can then be reused on any page within the site structure. To do this:

Library items are created as individual files with a "–.lib" extension.

1 Select an item in the Library

2 Drag and drop the selected Library item onto the Design view page

OR

Click on the Insert button on the Library panel

Once a Library item has been added to a document, it will remain there even if it is then subsequently deleted from the Library.

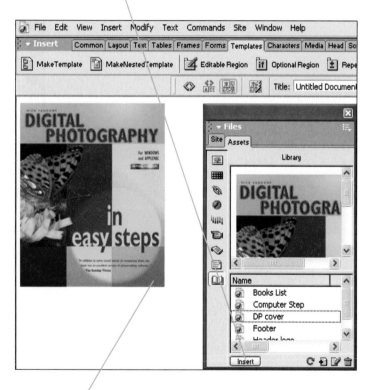

To change the color used to highlight Library items when they are placed in a document, select Edit>Preferences from the Menu bar, select Highlighting as the category and select a color from the box next to Library Items.

3 An instance of the Library item is placed on the page. This is locked, i.e. it cannot be edited in Design view and is highlighted by the color specified in the Highlighting section of the Preferences dialog box

Editing Library items

Library items are very versatile in that it is possible to edit them in the Library itself, in which case the changes apply to all of the instances of these items throughout the site, or individual Library items in a document can be made editable so that they can then be edited independently.

When a Library item is opened, it is done so in a separate window, with the words <<Library Item>> in the title.

Editing items in the Library

If you open and edit items in the Library itself, these changes can be applied to all occurrences of that item throughout a whole site. To do this:

1 Open an item in the Library by double-clicking the name or by clicking the Edit button

A Library item can also be edited by clicking on the arrow at the top of the Assets panel and selecting Edit from the menu.

2 In the Library Item window, make editing changes to the item. Select File>Save from the Menu bar to apply the changes

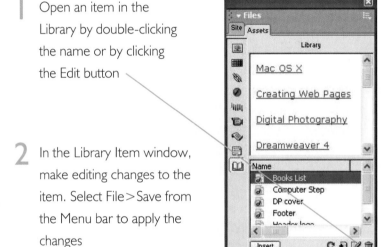

3 The Update Library Items dialog box will appear, asking if you want to update this item in all of the files in which it occurs. Click Update

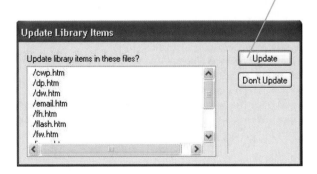

Editing Library items in a document

Once a Library item has been placed in a document it is still possible to perform certain editing tasks on it:

1   Select a Library item on a document page by clicking on it once. It will not be possible to edit this directly

2   The Library Properties box will be displayed

If an instance of a Library item is detached from the source document, then it loses all of the attributes it had previously. It no longer functions as a Library item.

Click Detach from Original to detach the item in the document from the source Library item. This means that it can be edited in the document window, but it will not have any changes applied to it if the source Library item is edited

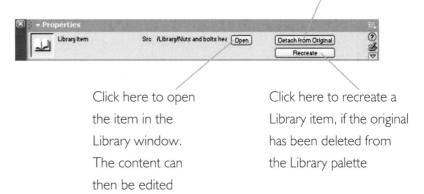

Click here to open the item in the Library window. The content can then be edited

Click here to recreate a Library item, if the original has been deleted from the Library palette

Creating editable navigation bars

A navigation bar is a set of buttons that can help the user navigate between the most commonly used areas or pages of a website. They can appear at the top or the side of all pages throughout a site. This has the advantage of creating a uniform style and it makes the user feel comfortable within the site. For information about creating navigation bars, see Chapter Seven, page 116. One of the possible drawbacks with navigation bars is that if you have them throughout your site and then decide to update a link within them, then it can be a laborious task. This can be greatly simplified by creating the navigation bar as a Library item:

If you have a site that contains a navigation bar on several hundred pages you will soon come to appreciate the importance of creating it as a Library item so that it can be updated site-wide in a single operation.

1 Create a navigation bar and convert it into a Library item by dragging it into one of the Library panels

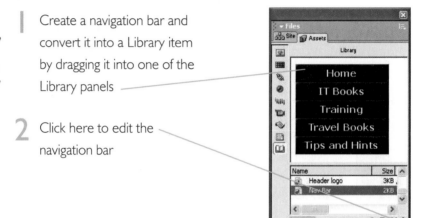

2 Click here to edit the navigation bar

After updating a Library item, make sure that all of the relevant files are uploaded to the remote site i.e. the one that is hosting the website.

3 Apply the editing changes and select File>Save from the Menu bar

4 You will be prompted as to whether you want to update all of the pages that contain this Library item. Click Update

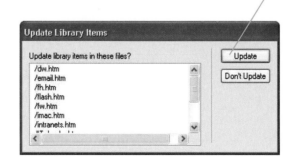

Adding text

This chapter looks at how to add text to Web pages and how to format its size and color. It also shows how to apply emphasis to text, align it, indent it, produce lists and use HTML styles.

Covers

Chapter Five

Text properties

Whenever text is being added or edited, the Text Properties Inspector is displayed. This shows the attributes of the current piece of text and it can be used to perform a variety of text formatting tasks:

If the Text Properties Inspector is not showing when you insert or edit text, select Window>Properties from the Menu bar.

Text format. Allows different styles to be applied to text   Font   Size   Color   Bold/Italic

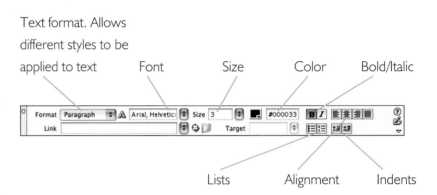

Lists   Alignment   Indents

The Text Properties Inspector also has options for creating textual hyperlinks to other pages or websites. This is looked at in more detail in Chapter Seven.

A lot of these commands can also be selected from the Menu bar and from the Text tab on the Insert panel:

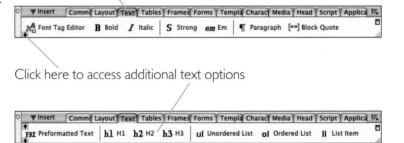

Click here to access additional text options

Fonts

There are literally hundreds of fonts available for use in creating Web pages. These range from the subdued and sombre to the weird and wacky. Generally, the fonts used on individual sites should be in keeping with the content of the site: a website for a firm of solicitors would probably contain different fonts to that for a cutting-edge design firm or a company selling computer games. The important factor about using fonts is consistency: use the same fonts for body text, headings and sub-headings throughout your site.

Fonts can be applied to existing items of text by selecting the text first, or a new font can be selected before you start inserting text. To select a font:

1 Click here to access the standard Dreamweaver list of the most commonly used fonts. Some options have three or four possibilities, in case the user's computer does not have the first choice. Click on one to select it

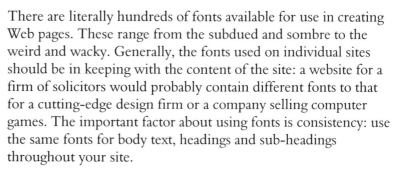

2 The selected font will be applied to any highlighted text and also any text that is inserted subsequently

Adding more fonts

There is no reason why you have to stick to the list of standard Dreamweaver fonts and you can add fonts that are stored on your own hard drive or from a CD-ROM:

If you choose an unusual or obscure font the person viewing your page will not be able to see the selected font unless they have it installed on their own computer. This means the text will be displayed in a similar font, or the browser default. Either way, it could look dramatically different from how you intended.

From the Text Properties Inspector font list select Edit Font List to add fonts to the standard list

> Default
> ✓ Arial, Helvetica, sans-serif
> Times New Roman, Times, serif
> Courier New, Courier, mono
> Georgia, Times New Roman, Times, serif
> Verdana, Arial, Helvetica, sans-serif
> Andale Mono
> Palatino
> Comic Sans MS
> Zapf Dingbats
> fantasy
> Edit Font List...

2 In the Edit Font List dialog box, click here to view the available fonts on your computer

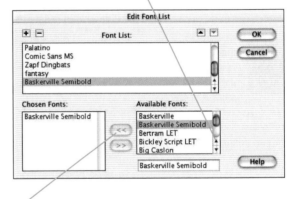

3 Click here to add a font to the Dreamweaver font list

4 The selected fonts are now available on the font list in the Text Properties Inspector

> Default
> ✓ Arial, Helvetica, sans-serif
> Times New Roman, Times, serif
> Courier New, Courier, mono
> Georgia, Times New Roman, Times, serif
> Verdana, Arial, Helvetica, sans-serif
> Andale Mono
> Palatino
> Comic Sans MS
> Zapf Dingbats
> fantasy
> Baskerville Semibold
>
> Edit Font List...

Size

The size of text can have just as important an impact on a Web page as the font. If used consistently, different sizes of text can be used to easily identify body text and different types of headings. The size of text can be changed manually, or by using preset format styles.

Changing size manually

A font size of 3 (the default size) in Dreamweaver, is equivalent to 12 point size in a word processing program.

1 Select a piece of text:

> **My writing career**
> I first began writing books after various far-flung places. When I

2 Click here in the Text Properties Inspector to access the options for changing the size

Format	Paragraph		🅰	Arial, Helvetic		Size	3	
Link						🌐 📁	Target	

3 Select a size for the text, ranging from 1 (smallest) to 7 (largest)

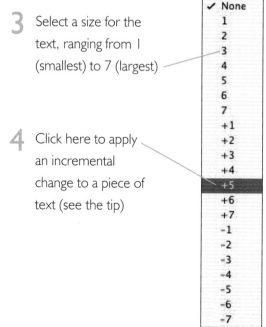

✓ None
1
2
3
4
5
6
7
+1
+2
+3
+4
+5
+6
+7
-1
-2
-3
-4
-5
-6
-7

The plus and minus values in the text size box are in relation to the default font size, which is equivalent to size 3. So +3 applied to a default size of text would be the same as applying size 6 to a piece of text. This can be used to vary the size of text, up to the equivalent of size 10.

4 Click here to apply an incremental change to a piece of text (see the tip)

Using Format styles

Text size and formatting can be specified using preset styles from either the Text Properties Inspector or the Text>Paragraph Format menu:

Formatting styles are applied to entire paragraphs i.e. all of the text between the <p></p> tags.

1 Insert the cursor within a paragraph that you want to format

My writing career
I first began writing books after about three various far-flung places. When I returned ho wrote four books about working and travellir and Getting a Job in Australia. Since then I which involves, among other things, workinç

2 Click here on the Text Properties Inspector to access the formatting options

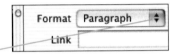

Format | Paragraph

Link

Once a formatting style has been applied, it is possible to apply further formatting to it, such as italics and alignment.

3 Select a formatting style. Heading 1 is the largest size of heading and Heading 6 is the smallest

✓ None	⌘0
Paragraph	⇧⌘P
Heading 1	⌘1
Heading 2	⌘2
Heading 3	⌘3
Heading 4	⌘4
Heading 5	⌘5
Heading 6	⌘6
Preformatted Text	

4 The selected style will be applied to the whole paragraph in which the cursor was inserted

Heading styles will only take effect if a size for the text has not already been selected in the font size box.

I first began writing books aft years of wandering around th various far-flung places. Whe home and finally hung up my

Color

Color is an excellent way to draw attention to text on a Web page. It can be used to highlight particular items or as a theme for consistent elements throughout a site. For instance, you could have all main headings in one color and the body text in another. However, do not get too carried away with using too many different colors on a single page: instead of creating an eye-catching and dynamic design you may just end up with a distracting rainbow effect. To add color to text:

Make sure that there is always a good contrast between text color and the background on which it appears e.g. black text on a white background. If the text color and the background are too similar, the text will be indistinct and difficult to read.

1 Select the text you want to recolor

The background color for a Web page can be set by selecting Modify>Page Properties from the Menu bar and selecting a color in the Background box.

2 Click here on the Text Properties Inspector to access the Text Color palette

3 Select a color in the palette. This will be displayed as a hexadecimal value

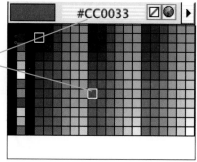

A hexadecimal value is a six character code that is used to display colors by defining how much red, green and blue they have. Hexadecimal values use numbers from 1–9 and letters from A–F.

4 The selected color is displayed here in the Text Properties Inspector and its hexadecimal value is displayed next to it

Emphasis and alignment

Two further ways of formatting text are adding bold and italics for emphasis and adjusting the alignment on the page.

Bold and italics

Bold and italics can also be applied by selecting a piece of text and pressing Ctrl+B (Windows) or Command+B (Mac) and Ctrl+I (Windows) or Command+I (Mac) respectively.

| Select a piece of text

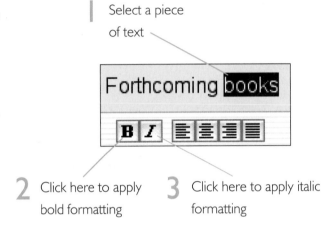

2 Click here to apply bold formatting

3 Click here to apply italic formatting

Alignment

Text can be aligned with even greater precision through the use of tables. The text can be placed within the cells of a table and then have the alignment functions listed here applied to it. For more information about tables, see Chapter Eight.

| Select a piece of text

2 Click here to left-align the text

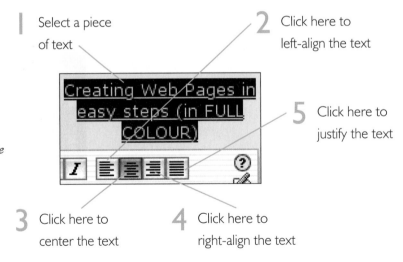

5 Click here to justify the text

3 Click here to center the text

4 Click here to right-align the text

Lists

There are functions for producing bulleted and numbered lists and also for indenting lines or paragraphs of text.

Lists

Lists can be used to break up long passages of text, or convey complicated arguments more clearly. Bulleted lists should be used if all of the points are of equal importance, while numbered lists can be used for items of varying importance.

1 Select a piece of text

2 Click here to create a numbered list

3 Click here to create a bulleted list

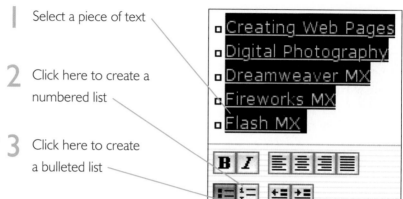

Further list formatting options

*Lists can only be created with items that are separated by paragraph breaks i.e. <p> tags, rather than line breaks i.e.
 tags.*

1 Select part of a list

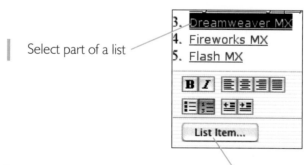

2 Click on the List Item button in the Text Properties Inspector

3 Select the options in the List Properties dialog box and click OK

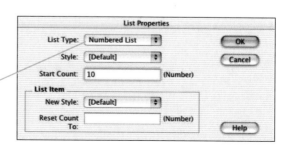

Indents

The indenting option can be used to move text to the left or the right and also create nested lists i.e. lists within lists:

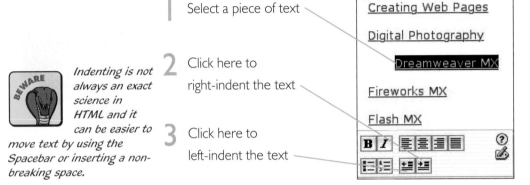

Indenting is not always an exact science in HTML and it can be easier to move text by using the Spacebar or inserting a non-breaking space.

1 Select a piece of text

2 Click here to right-indent the text

3 Click here to left-indent the text

Creating nested lists

Left indents can only be used if an item has already been right-indented.

1 Select part of an existing list or insert the cursor within a list

- Creating Web Pages
- Digital Photography
- Dreamweaver MX
- Fireworks MX
- Flash MX

2 Click on the right-indent button to nest the list to the next level

- Creating Web Pages
- Digital Photography
  - Dreamweaver MX
- Fireworks MX
- Flash MX

Indents are denoted in the HTML source code with the `<blockquote>` `</blockquote>` tags.

3 Repeat the process if any further levels of nesting are required

- Creating Web Pages
- Digital Photography
    - Dreamweaver MX
- Fireworks MX
- Flash MX

HTML styles

When you are designing a website, consistency is important. This not only helps the user feel confident about moving around your site, in the knowledge that the layout and format will be familiar from page to page, but it also creates a professional image. Having consistently formatted text is one of the key areas in this respect and it is one that can cause problems if you try and format every piece of text manually. Unless you are painstakingly careful, you will probably miss some items that should have been formatted differently.

HTML styles are similar in their operation to those used in word processing and desktop publishing programs.

To help the designer gain consistency with the textual elements of a site, Dreamweaver has a function called HTML styles. This lets you set predefined styles for items such as body text and headings, which can then be applied to the text within your site. This not only helps with the consistency of a site, it is also a quick way to format a lot of text. Styles can be created within the HTML Styles panel and then applied to text.

Creating HTML styles

To create new HTML styles:

1 Click on the HTML Styles panel tab

2 The current list of styles is listed in the HTML Styles panel

A new style can also be created by clicking on the down pointing arrow on the HTML Styles panel and selecting New.

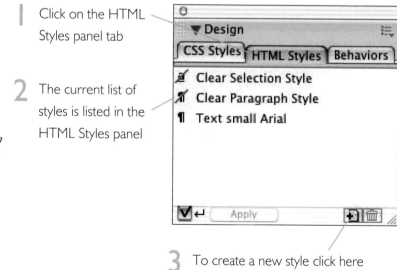

3 To create a new style click here

4 Double-click on the text in the Name box and give your new style a name, such as "Sub-heading"

If a style is to be applied to a selection it will only affect text that has been highlighted. If it is to be applied to a paragraph then the cursor only has to be inserted anywhere in the required paragraph. The style will then affect the whole paragraph.

5 Click these options on or off to determine whether the style will be applied to a whole paragraph or just text that has been selected, and whether it will overwrite an existing style or not

6 Select formatting attributes for the new style

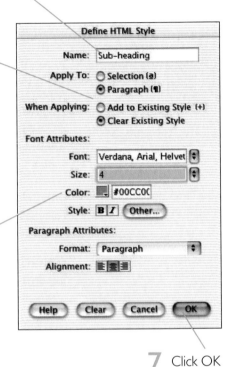

7 Click OK

Styles can be deleted by selecting them in the HTML Styles panel and then clicking on the Wastebasket icon in the bottom right corner of the panel.

Applying styles

To apply a style to text:

1 Select a piece of text or insert the cursor in a paragraph

2 Apply a style by clicking on it once in the HTML Styles panel

Working with images

Images can be a powerful design tool on a Web page, as long as they are used economically and effectively. This chapter gives an overview of using images on the Web and explains how to use them in Dreamweaver. It also shows how to create rollover images.

Covers

Chapter Six

Web image overview

When the Web was first being developed it was considered to be a significant achievement to transfer plain, unformatted, text from one computer to another. However, things have moved on considerably from then and the Web is now awash with complex graphics, animations and sounds, to name but a few of the multimedia effects that are now available to the Web designer.

Despite the range of items that can be used on Web pages, graphics are still by far the most popular. These can include photographic images, icons, clip art and even animated graphics. These are all important design elements for Web pages and they should not be overlooked when you are creating a new website.

If you use an image editing program, such as Macromedia Fireworks, images can be optimized so that the best quality can be matched with the smallest file size.

When graphical formats were being developed for the Web there was a need to create good quality images that were still small enough to allow them to be downloaded quickly onto the user's computer. This resulted in two file formats that offer good quality while still creating small file sizes. These are Graphical Interchange Format (GIF) and Joint Photographic Experts Group (JPEG). Some points to bear in mind about both of these formats:

- JPEGs use up to 16 million colors and so are best suited for photographic images

- GIFs use 256 colors and so are best suited for images that do not contain a lot of color definition, such as images with blocks of similar color

The two types of compression that are used with image file formats are lossy and lossless. With lossy compression some image quality is lost, while with lossless compression it is retained. JPEGs use lossy compression while PNGs use lossless compression.

- One variety of GIF (GIF 89a) can be used to create images with transparent backgrounds

- Both GIFs and JPEGs use forms of compression to make the file size smaller

Another, more recent, image format for the Web is PNG (Portable Network Group). It uses 16 million colors and lossless compression. There are a couple of points to consider with PNGs:

- Not all browsers support the PNG format

- PNG files can contain meta-tags, indexing information that can be read by Web search engines when someone is looking for your website

Using images effectively

When you use a program such as Dreamweaver, which gives you the power to quickly and easily insert images into Web pages, the temptation is to add them at every opportunity. However, this should be resisted as it is important to use images carefully and make the most of their impact and design potential. Some points to bear in mind when using images on Web pages are:

- The more images you include, the longer it will take for the user to download your site i.e. access it from the host server. This can cause a real problem, because most Web users do not have the patience to wait a long time for pages to download. This can be measured in seconds rather than minutes

- Images can be used as the background to a Web page or as independent items within it. Either way, the file size of the image will determine the downloading time

- Keep the onscreen size of images small. Again, this can affect the downloading time and it can detract from other content on a page

- Do not overuse images that spin, blink or flicker. While this can create a positive initial effect, it can become extremely irritating after it has been viewed several times

- Use images for a specific purpose, i.e. to convey information or as a design feature

- Do not use images that could be deemed offensive or derogatory to any individuals or groups

- Use the same image, or groups of images, to achieve a consistent look throughout a website

- Do not use images just for the sake of it, or just because you can. Users will soon realize that the images are not serving a useful purpose

- Do not use images at the expense of core information. Users may want to find a piece of contact information rather than look at a lot of images

Do not make your website too dependant on images, since users can set their browsers so that they do not display any graphics.

Inserting images

Obtaining images

Images for insertion in a website can be obtained from a variety of sources:

- System clip art collections (most computers come with some items of clip art already pre-installed)

- CD-ROMs. There are several CD-ROMs on the market that contain tens of thousands of graphical and photographic images

For a detailed look at digital cameras and digital images, take a look at "Digital Photography in easy steps".

- Digital cameras. These are affordable for the home user and offer a versatile option for creating your own images for a Web page

- Scanners. These can be used to capture existing images in a digital format

Inserting images

To use an image for the background of a page, select Modify>Page Properties from the Menu bar. Click on the Browse button next to the Background Image box and select an image in the same way as for inserting it directly onto a page.
To create a watermark effect, use an image editing program to make the image semi-transparent and then insert it as the background.

1 Insert the cursor at the point on the page where you want the image and click on the Image button on the Common tab on the Insert panel

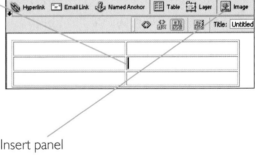

2 Locate the image you want to use and click on OK (Windows) or Choose (Mac)

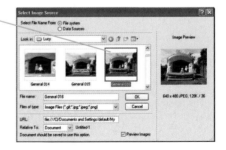

Image properties

When an image is selected in Dreamweaver, the Properties Inspector displays information about that image. To access the Image Properties Inspector:

When an image is inserted on a page in Dreamweaver, this is only really a reference to where the image is physically located on your computer, rather than the image itself being physically inserted. This is denoted by the <src> tag.

1   Select an image by clicking on it once

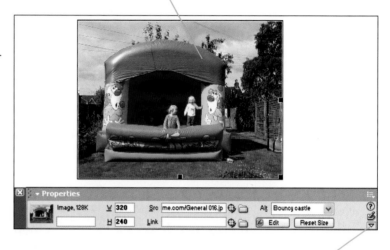

Using Alternative (Alt) text in place of an image is important for people who choose not to view images or who are visually impaired and use a reader to view the Web. Type a description of the image in the Alt box. This can be a couple of words or several sentences.

2   The Image Properties Inspector is activated. Click here to expand it to view all of the options

File details   Image dimensions   Image location   Alternative text

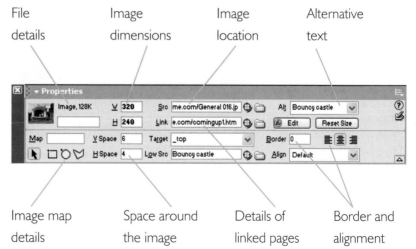

Image map details   Space around the image   Details of linked pages   Border and alignment

Resizing images

If possible, try and resize images in an image editing program, such as Fireworks, before they are inserted into a Dreamweaver document.

Even if you have sized an image in an image editing program before it is inserted into a Dreamweaver document, there is a good chance that it will not be exactly the right size for your purposes. To resize an image:

1   Select an image by clicking on it once

2   Drag the midpoint resizing handles to change the horizontal or vertical size independently of each other, or the corner handle to change the horizontal and vertical size simultaneously (hold down Shift to resize proportionately)

Do not resize images too many times, or else the image quality will deteriorate.
The quality will be better if you decrease the size of the image rather than increase it.

3   Instead of Step 2, enter values in the Image Properties Inspector to alter the height and width of the image

Aligning images and text

During the process of creating a website, there will be several occasions where you will want to combine images and text. This could be to include a textual definition of an image or to wrap a block of text around an image, in the style of a newspaper or a magazine article. This can be done through the use of various Dreamweaver functions (see the HOT TIP) or an image can have a value assigned to it so that it deals with text alignment in a certain way. To align an image and text together:

One of the most versatile ways of aligning and laying out images and text is through the use of tables. This will enable you to produce precision alignment. The alignment options on this page can also be applied to images and text once they are inserted into a table. For more on tables, see Chapter Eight.

1 Select an image by clicking on it once. It can already have text around it, or the text can be added later:

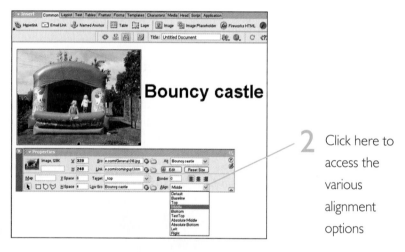

2 Click here to access the various alignment options

The baseline of a text block is the line on which the bottom of most of the letters sit. This does not include descenders (such as in "g" and "j") which extend below the baseline.

The options for aligning images and text are:

- Browser default. This varies with browsers but it usually aligns the text baseline with the image base

- Baseline. This aligns the baseline with the image base

- Top. This aligns the tallest point of the text with the top of the image

- Middle. This aligns the text baseline with the middle of the image

- Bottom. This aligns the baseline of the text with the bottom of the image

- Text Top. This aligns the tallest point of the text with the top of the image

- Absolute Middle. This aligns the middle of the text block with the middle of the image

- Absolute Bottom. This aligns the bottom of the text, including descenders, with the bottom of the image

- Left. This places the image to the left of any text that is next to it. The text will then wrap around the image

- Right. This places the image to the right of any text that is next to it

Aligning images and text can create some interesting, and sometimes unwanted, effects. Experiment with different settings until you feel confident about each combination.

Alignment buttons

As well as using the alignment options described above, it is also possible to align images and text by using the alignment buttons in the Image Properties Inspector. Even though this is done by selecting an image, the alignment is applied to the text:

Image with the Left-alignment option and the Align Left button

Image with the Middle-alignment option and the Align Center button

Another use for images is the Trace option. This is where a design has been created and is then inserted onto a Web page as a background for the Web designer to copy, or trace over. The trace image does not appear on the published page and it is really a guide for the Web designer to follow.

To use a trace image, select Modify>Page Properties from the Menu bar and in the Tracing Image box select the trace image as you would for any other image. There are also options for applying certain levels of transparency.

Creating rollover images

One of the most eye-catching effects with images on the Web is the creation of rollovers. This is where two images are combined, although only one is visible initially on the page. However, when the cursor is moved over the image, it is replaced by the second one. To make this even more impressive, a hyperlink can be added to the rollover so that the user can click on it and they will be taken to another page within the site, or a different site altogether.

Do not get too carried away with using rollovers, although this can be difficult to resist when you first learn how to create them. As with any item on a Web page that moves or changes from one thing to another, a little goes a long way.

Until recently, rollovers were the preserve of designers who could use programming languages such as Javascript. However, Dreamweaver overcomes this by allowing you to create rollovers, while generating all of the script in the background. This means that you have a powerful design tool at your disposal, without having to delve into computer language scripting.

Creating a rollover image

Create the two images that you want to use for the rollover. Make sure they are the same dimensions because they will be produced as the same size in the rollover

If you are using a rollover to link to another page or site on the Web, choose your images carefully so that the user can quickly relate the image with the link that it contains. Otherwise, they may think that it is just a clever graphical effect.

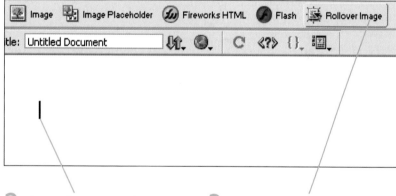

2 Insert the cursor where you want the rollover to appear

3 On the Common tab on the Insert panel, click the Rollover Image button

Click here to enter a name for the rollover button

One effective device is to use the same image for both the initial image and the rollover one. However, edit the rollover image to be a different color, or some degree of transparency. This will then produce a subtle effect when the rollover is activated.

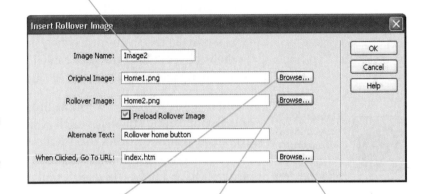

5 Click here to locate the first image you're going to use. Repeat the process by clicking here for the second image

URL stands for Uniform Resource Locator and it is a unique address for every page on the Web. It is usually in a format similar to `http://www.mysite.com`

If you are linking to a page on your own site, you only need to insert the page name i.e. news.htm. But if you want to link to an external website, you will need to insert the full URL, which can be copied from the Address bar in the browser when you are viewing the page.

6 If you want the user to be able to go to another Web page when they click, click here to select a page to link to. Click OK to create the rollover

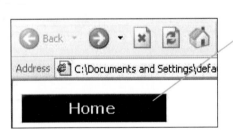

7 When viewed in a browser, the image will look like this initially...

...and this when the cursor moves over it

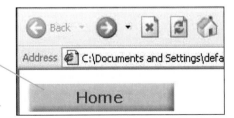

To test a rollover, save the file and press F12 or select File>Preview in Browser from the Menu bar.

Using hyperlinks

This chapter looks at how items on Web pages can be linked together through the use of hyperlinks. It shows how to create links to other Web pages and also to items within the same page. It also demonstrates how to create image maps and navigation bars.

Covers

Chapter Seven

About hyperlinks

Without hyperlinks (or just links), the Web would be an unconnected collection of pages and sites that would be tortuous to navigate around since you would have to specify the Web address (URL) for each page that you wanted to view. Hyperlinks simplify this process considerably: they are pieces of HTML coding that create "clickable" regions on a Web page i.e. the user can click on a hyperlink and it will take them to the linked item. In simple terms, hyperlinks are shortcuts for jumping between elements on the Web.

URL stands for Uniform Resource Locator and it refers to the unique address of every page on the Web.

Both text and images can be used as hyperlinks: text usually appears underlined when it is acting as a hyperlink and, for both elements, the cursor turns into a pointing hand when it is positioned over a hyperlink on a Web page.

The code for a simple hyperlink to a page within the same site structure could look like this:

<a href="news.htm">Latest News</a>

Some of the items hyperlinks can be linked to include other pages within the same website, other locations on the same page, other websites and email addresses.

In this example the words "Latest News" would be underlined on the page and when the user clicks on them, the page "news.htm" will open.

Types of hyperlinks

There are different types of hyperlinks depending on what they are linking to:

- Absolute links. These are links that go externally to other pages on the Web. This means that the full URL has to be inserted so the browser knows where to look i.e. `http://www.macromedia.com/software/dreamweaver/`

For relative links, the notation "../" in a hyperlink address means move up one level in the folder hierarchy and "/" means move down one level.

- Relative links. These are links to files within the same site structure. This would appear in the following format:
  <a href="main.htm">My Day</a>

- Email links. These are links to specific email addresses. These are created with the following code as the link:
  <a href="mailto:nickvandome@hotmail.com"> Nick Vandome</a>

Linking to documents

Links can be created to a variety of documents, including images, sounds and video clips, but the most common type of link is to another Web page. Dreamweaver provides a number of ways to achieve this:

Using the Properties Inspector

If you are using images as hyperlinks, make sure that they are clearly identifiable, otherwise the user may think they are just a graphical design feature.

1 Select an image or piece of text which you want to make into a link

2 Click here and enter the URL of the page to which you want to link

OR

Click here to browse your hard drive for a file to link to. Once you have chosen one, click on OK (Windows) or Choose (Mac)

If you browse to a file outside your current site structure, and try and link to it, a warning box will appear alerting you to the fact that the file is not contained within the current structure. You will be given the option of then saving it within the current structure. This will ensure that the link is correct.

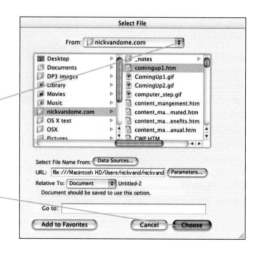

3 The selected file will now be visible here in the Properties Inspector

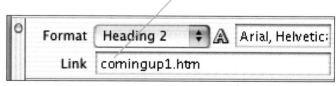

Using the Menu bar

Links can also be created by right-clicking (Windows) or Ctrl+clicking (Mac) on the selected object and selecting Make Link from the contextual menu.

Hyperlinks can be edited or removed by selecting the link, clicking on Modify>Change Link (or Remove Link) from the Menu bar and selecting a new file from your hard drive.

Alternatively, right-click (Windows) or Ctrl+click (Mac) on a link and select Change Link (or Remove Link) from the contextual menu.

Select an image or piece of text which you want to make into a link

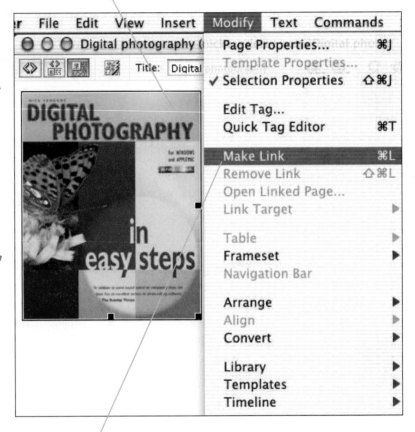

Select Modify>Make Link from the Menu bar and select a file as shown on the previous page

Linking to anchors

As well as being able to create hyperlinks to other pages within your own site, and external sites, it is also possible to use links to move about the same page. This can be particularly useful if you have a lot of text on a page, or several sections, and you want to enable the users to navigate around the page without having to scroll down the page too much. In Dreamweaver this is done through the use of anchors. These are inserted on the page at the required points and hyperlinks are then created to them from other parts of the page. To do this:

Anchors are also known as bookmarks in other Web authoring programs.

1 Insert the cursor at the point where you want the anchor to appear

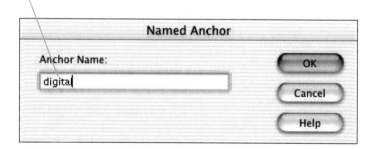

It is not necessary to select an image or a piece of text when creating an anchor. The anchor is independent of any other item on the page and is placed at the insertion point of the cursor.

2 Select Insert>Named Anchor from the Menu bar

3 In the Named Anchor dialog box, type a name for the anchor. This is the name that will be used in the link to the anchor. Click OK

When naming anchors, give them a single name. It is possible to enter more than one name in the dialog box, but this can cause problems when the link is trying to find the specified anchor.

4 The anchor will be denoted on the page by this element.

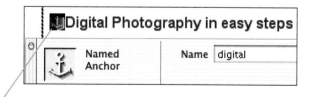

Click on it to see the anchor's properties

5 Select the image or piece of text on the page that is going to act as the link to the named anchor

If you are using a lot of anchors on a page, it is advisable to include links back to the top of the page. This means that the user will not feel lost in the middle of a long document.

To include a link back to the beginning of a document, insert an anchor at the top of the page and name it Top. Then move further down the document and type Top or Top of Page. Select the text and create a hyperlink to #top. When clicked, this should then take the user to the Top anchor at the beginning of the document.

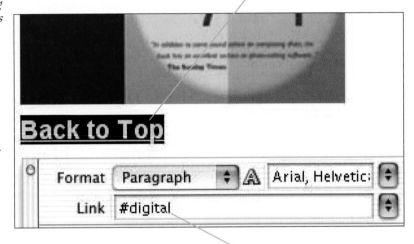

6 In the Properties Inspector, enter the name of the anchor here, preceded by the # symbol

7 It is also possible to link to an anchor in another document, in which case the full filename should be inserted here, followed by # and the anchor name as above

Press F12 or select File> Preview in Browser to test the page in a browser and make sure that the link goes to the correct anchor.

Creating an email link

To create a link that allows the user to access an email address, first insert the cursor at the point where you want the link to appear, then:

1 Click on the Email Link button on the Common tab on the Insert panel

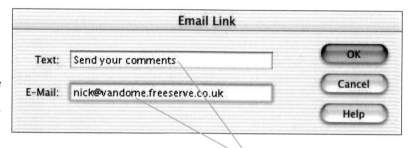

If you include an email link on your site, it is a good idea to include some form of privacy statement, saying that you will not pass on any email addresses that you receive as a result of a message that is sent to you. Unfortunately, there are some unscrupulous individuals who do this sort of thing, resulting in the people being deluged with junk email.

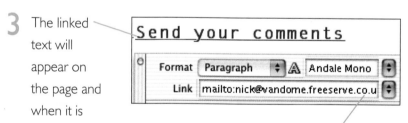

2 In the Email Link dialog box, insert the text that will be displayed for the link and enter the email address to which the link will point. Click OK

3 The linked text will appear on the page and when it is selected the email address to which it is linked will be shown in the Properties Inspector. When the link is activated in a browser, the user's email program will open, with the address pre-inserted in the To box

Point-to-File links

When you are creating links, there may be times when you do not want to insert the filename of the document to which you want to link, but rather just point to a file and instruct Dreamweaver to link to that item. With the innovative Point-to-File tool you can do just that. Dreamweaver even lets you use it in several different ways.

Point-to-File in the document window

The Point-to-File tool can be used to link two files that have both been opened in the document window:

The Point-to-File technique cannot be used to create links to external Web pages, even if they are opened next to the document window.

To position two documents next to each other on the screen select Window>Tile Horizontally (or Tile Vertically) from the Menu bar.

1 Resize the two open files so that they are both visible in the document window

2 Select the image or piece of text which you want to use as the link

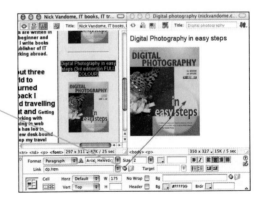

3 Click here in the Properties Inspector and drag the cursor into the file to be linked to

4 The item selected in Step 2 is now linked to the other document

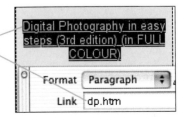

Point-to-File in the site window

 If you want to link a lot of different files, doing so with the Point-to-File tool in the site window could be the quickest way. However, it would be advisable to draw out a rough sketch of how you want the linked structure to look.

1 Select Site > Site Map from the Menu bar

2 Select a file in the Site Map window

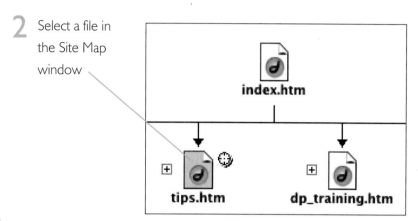

 For more information about accessing with the Site Map, see Chapter Two, page 37.

3 Click on this icon and drag to one of the files in the Local Files list

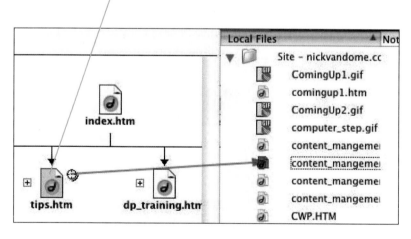

The link that is inserted into the target file is a plain text one, consisting of the page's filename. This can be edited by opening the file in a document window.

4 A textual link will automatically be inserted in the file from which the Point-to-File link was dragged

Point-to-File for anchors

1 Insert an anchor and select an item that is going to link to it

If you are using the Point-to-File technique to link to an anchor that is not visible on screen, the page will automatically scroll up or down as you drag the Point-to-File arrow.

2 Hold down Shift and drag the cursor from the selected item to the anchor. An arrow will appear as you drag

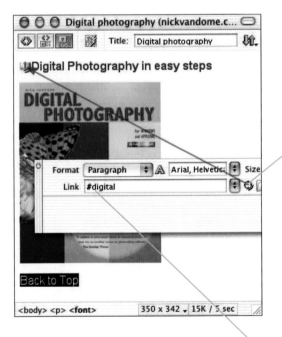

3 Or, click here on the Properties Inspector and drag until the arrow is positioned over the anchor, then release

4 The link will have been made to the named anchor

Image maps

An image map is a device that allows you to insert links to multiple files within a single image. Links within an image map are created with "hotspots" which are drawn over an image. Image maps can be used with any image that has easily identifiable areas. To create an image map:

1 Insert the image that is going to serve as the image map and select it by clicking on it once

2 In the Properties Inspector, click on one of the Hotspot tools

3 Draw an area on the image that is going to act as a hotspot. This is the area which the user will be able to click on and jump to the linked file

4 After a hotspot has been drawn, enter a file to link to here, or browse to select a file from your hard drive

Navigation bars

One of the best devices for moving around a website is a navigation bar. This is a set of buttons that contain links to the other main areas of the site. Once a navigation bar has been created, it can be stored and placed on as many pages as required.

When a navigation bar is created, each button can have a different image assigned to it depending on its state i.e. how it is interacting with the cursor (see the HOT TIP). To create a navigation bar:

1 Create the images that you want to use for the various states of the buttons in the navigation bar and click on the Navigation Bar button on the Common tab on the Insert panel

2 Name the first element of the navigation bar

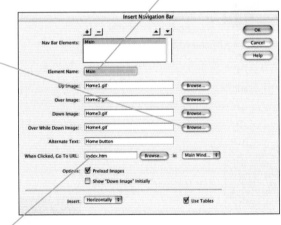

3 Click the Browse buttons to select the images that are going to be used for each state of the button

4 Click here to enter the page to which the button will link

6 Click OK

5 Click **+** to add each button to the navigation bar. Repeat Steps 2–4 for each button you want to include on the navigation bar

Tables and Layout view

This chapter shows how tables can be used to format the content of Web pages. It explains how to create tables, edit and format them and also how to add content and even create tables within tables. It also explains how Layout view can be used with tables to create complex layouts that will appear consistent in all browsers.

Covers

Chapter Eight

Designing with tables

One of the biggest challenges for any Web designer is to create a page layout that is both versatile and visually appealing. This invariably involves combining text and images and, before the advent of tables in HTML, it was a considerable problem trying to get everything in the right place. Even when elements looked correct on the designer's computer, there was no guarantee that they would appear the same when viewed on different computers and with different browsers. However, tables changed all that.

HTML tables are one of the most important design tools that are available to Web authors. Although their name suggests that they should perhaps only mainly be used to collate and display figures, this is definitely not the case: tables can contain the same content that is placed at any other point on a HTML page. They can then be used to position different elements and, since each item can be placed in its own individual cell within the table, the designer can be confident that this is the position in which they will appear, regardless of the browser used.

Tables can be used for simple formatting techniques, such as aligning text and images, or they can be used to display a whole page of complex design:

HTML tables are made up of a grid for the whole table, into which are placed rows and cells. The HTML code for these is:

- Table – <table> </table>
- Row – <tr> </tr>
- Cell – <td> </td>

If the borders of a table are made invisible, i.e. set to 0, the user will not be aware that the content on the page is inside a table. This can make complex designs look even more impressive.

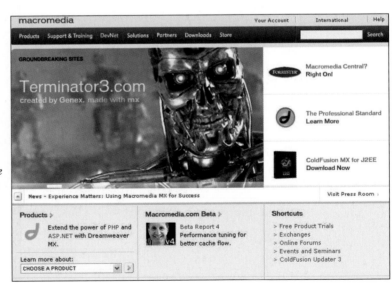

Inserting a table

You can insert as many tables as you like on a page and tables can also be nested i.e. tables placed within other tables. This provides even more versatility in the design process. When a table is inserted, various attributes can be set initially. However, it is also possible to edit and amend a table's attributes at any time after it has been created. To insert a table:

Tables can also be created by selecting Insert>Table from the Menu bar. This brings up the same dialog box as using the Insert panel.

1   On the Common tab on the Insert panel, click on the Table button

2   Enter the number of rows and columns that are required for the table

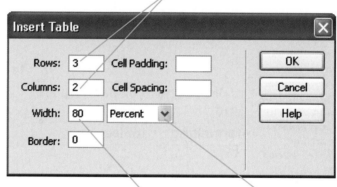

Use the percentage setting for the width of a table if you want to make sure it will all fit in the user's browser. However this could affect the way some of the content is displayed within the table. Use the pixel setting if you want the formatting to remain exactly as it has been designed.

3   Enter a value for the size of the table. Click here to select a percentage size or a pixel size. If it is a percentage size, this will always appear as a percentage of the browser window in which it is being viewed. The pixel size is the actual physical size of the table

4 Enter a size for the table border. A value of 0 will create an invisible border and the default value is 1

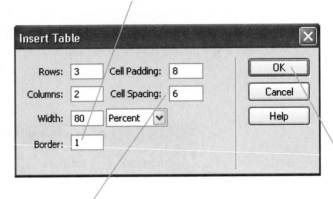

5 Enter values for the Cell Padding and the Cell Spacing. Cell padding affects how much space there is around each item in a cell and cell spacing affects how much space there is between the cells in a table

6 Click OK to create the table

If the cell padding is increased, the size of the individual cells increases too, since the area for adding content in the cell is still the same, it is just the area around it that increases. If the cell spacing is increased the size of the cells decreases, to accommodate the space around them.

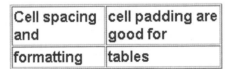

Cell spacing and	cell padding are good for
formatting	tables

A table with cell padding and cell spacing both at 1

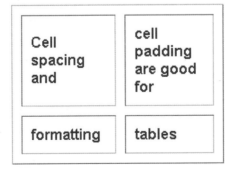

Cell spacing and	cell padding are good for
formatting	tables

A table with cell padding and cell spacing both at 10

Editing a table

If you create a table and then decide you want to change some of its attributes, then it is possible to do so through the Properties Inspector. In addition to the settings that can be used in the Insert Table dialog box, there are also some additional attributes that can be used:

1 Click once on a table's bottom or right border, or the top left corner, to select it. A thick black line with 3 resizing handles should appear around it

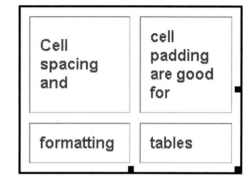

Cell spacing and	cell padding are good for
formatting	tables

The resizing handles which appear when a table is selected can be used to change the dimensions of the table by dragging. The handle on the bottom resizes the table vertically, the one on the right side resizes it horizontally and the one in the right corner resizes it both vertically and horizontally. Hold down Shift while dragging this button to change the dimensions proportionally.

It is not essential to name tables, but it is a good way to keep track of them if you are using a lot that contain similar items of information.

2 Once a table is selected the Table Properties Inspector will appear:

3 Enter a name for the table here

4 Enter values for the number of rows and columns, width and height and cell padding and cell spacing, in the same way as when the table was created

5 Click here to access options for aligning the table on the page: this can be Left, Center or Right

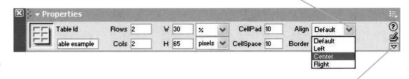

If you select an image as the background for a table, make sure it does not detract from the content of the table itself.

6 Click here to access additional table properties – see below

7 Clear cell height or width

Pixels can be used if you want to create a fixed-width table, i.e. one where the content retains its format whatever the size of the window in which it is being viewed. Depending on the design, this can result in the user having to scroll left and right to see the whole page.

Percent can be used if you want the table to always take up a certain portion of the screen. This can result in the content on the page becoming distorted from the original design.

8 Change the table height or width to pixels or percent

9 Click here to select a background color for the table (left box) and an outer border color (right box)

10 Click here to select an image for the table background

Rows and columns

When tables are being used, particularly for complex designs, it is unlikely that the correct number of rows and columns will be specified first time. As shown on page 121, it is possible to add or delete the number of rows and columns by selecting the table and amending the values in the Table Properties Inspector. This can also be achieved as follows:

1 Insert the cursor in the table where you want to add or delete rows or columns. Right-click (Windows) or Ctrl+click (Mac) and select Table

2 Insert a single row or column by selecting Insert Row or Insert Column

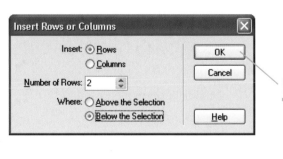

3 To insert multiple rows or columns, click Insert Rows or Columns and follow step 4

4 In the dialog box, enter whether you want to insert rows or columns, the number to be inserted and where you want them placed in relation to the insertion point:

Rows and columns can also be inserted or deleted by inserting the cursor in the table (but not selecting the table) and selecting Modify>Table from the Menu bar.

Rows and columns can be resized by following steps 1 and 2 and then selecting Increase Row Span, Increase Column Span, Decrease Row Span or Decrease Column Span from the contextual menu. They can also be resized by dragging the relevant row or column border.

5 Click OK to insert the specified number of rows or columns

Selecting cells

Once a table has been created it can be useful to select individual cells, or groups of cells, so that specific formatting options can be applied to them. For instance, you may want to have a table where the top row of cells is a different size or color to the rest of the cells in the table. Or you may want to apply separate formatting options to single cells.

If the cell you are trying to select is in the first column of a table, you have to drag the cursor to the right-hand border of the cell. If it is in the last column of a table, you have to drag the cursor to the left-hand border of the cell. If the cell you are trying to select is in any other column in the table, it can be selected by dragging the cursor to the left- or right-hand border. The same applies for selecting a cell within rows in a table.

Selecting cells

Insert the cursor in the cell you want to select, hold and drag to the outer border of the cell. A thick dark line appears around the cell to indicate it has been selected. To select more than one cell, keep dragging until all of the required cells have been covered

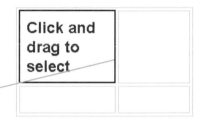

Merging cells

Once cells have been selected, it is then possible to merge them together, independently of the other cells in the table. This is an excellent formatting device as it allows the designer to break the symmetrical pattern of a table, which gives increased flexibility. To merge cells once they have been selected:

Entire rows and columns can be selected by positioning the cursor on the relevant border until a thick black arrow appears and clicking once.

1 With the required cells selected, right-click (Windows) or Ctrl+click (Mac) and select Table>Merge Cells

Cells can also be merged by selecting them and then selecting Modify>Table>Merge Cells from the Menu bar.

2 Or click here on the Properties Inspector

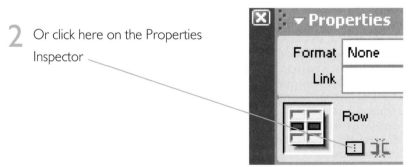

3 The selected cells are now merged independently of the other cells in the table

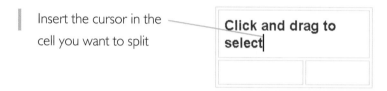

Splitting cells

Any cell within a table can be split into smaller parts, regardless of whether it has already been merged or not. To do this:

The Split Cell option is only available if you select a single cell. If you try and activate this command when more than one cell is selected it will be grayed out i.e. unavailable.

1 Insert the cursor in the cell you want to split

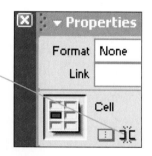

2 Right-click (Windows) or Ctrl+click (Mac) and select Table>Split Cell from the contextual menu

3 Or click here on the Properties Inspector

If you split a cell that contains content i.e. text or images, this will be placed in the left-hand cell if the cell is split by columns, and the top cell if it is split by rows.

4 In the Split Cell dialog box, select whether you want to split the cell into rows and columns and the required number. Click OK

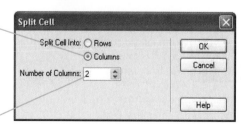

Adding content

If an item can be added to a page within Dreamweaver, then it can be inserted in a table too. A table acts only as a placeholder for content; it does not determine the type of content which it can display.

Adding text

If you are including text and images in the same cell, insert a paragraph break <p> </p> between them. This will make it possible to align them independently of each other, if required.

1 Insert the cursor in the cell in which you want to include the text

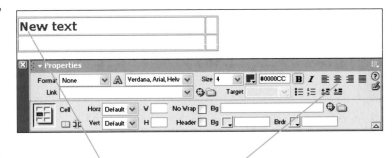

If you are including text and images in the same cell, make sure the No Wrap option is not checked on. Otherwise the text will continue to fill the cell, and keep expanding it, rather than move onto the next line.

2 Enter the text and click on one of these buttons in the Properties Inspector to align it

Adding images and more

Images, and most forms of multimedia content, can also be added to a table:

1 Insert the cursor in the cell in which you want to insert the image or other media

If an image is larger than the cell it is being inserted into, the cell will automatically expand to accommodate the item. This could have the effect of distorting the rest of the cells in the table.

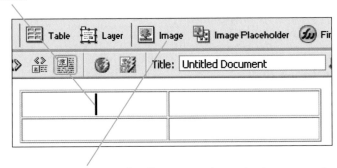

2 Click on the Image button on the Common tab on the Insert panel and select an item from your hard drive

Aligning items in a table

Both text and images can be aligned by using the alignment buttons on the Table Properties Inspector. However, it is also possible to apply alignment settings to an entire cell. To do this:

If you specify settings for cell alignment and then use the alignment buttons in the Properties Inspector, this will override the cell alignment settings. It is best to use one method or the other within individual cells.

1 Insert the cursor in a cell and click here to specify the horizontal alignment that you want applied to the cell

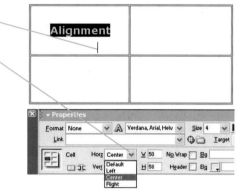

The default settings for cell alignment are horizontal as left and vertical as middle.

2 Click here to specify the vertical alignment that you want applied to the cell

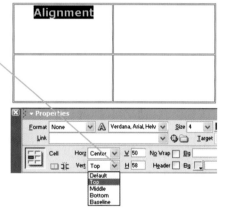

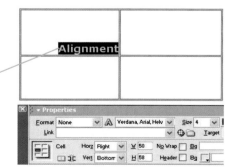

Using the vertical and horizontal alignment options is an excellent way to center items within a cell, something that could not be done with the same accuracy using the alignment buttons.

3 Any content that is in the cell, or is added to it, will take on the specified alignment settings

Creating nested tables

The full versatility of using tables for formatting comes when you start inserting tables within tables, or creating nested tables. This can create highly complex designs and, if all of the borders are set to 0, it can be hard for the user to tell that tables are being used at all; they just see a page with a highly sophisticated degree of formatting. To create nested tables:

Merge cells within nested tables to give even greater versatility to your design.

Preset designs can be applied to any table by selecting Commands> Format Table from the Menu bar and selecting one of the available designs.

1 Click on the Table button on the Common tab on the Insert panel

2 Specify the settings for your initial table. Click OK

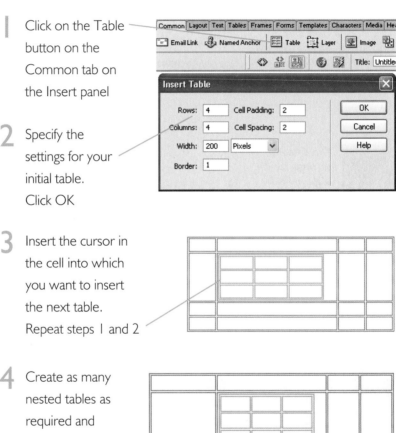

3 Insert the cursor in the cell into which you want to insert the next table. Repeat steps 1 and 2

4 Create as many nested tables as required and then start adding content to your design

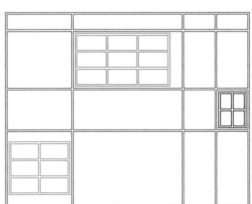

Layout view

Despite their versatility for design purposes, traditional HTML tables can sometimes be difficult to format exactly as you want them. This has been an occasional problem with Dreamweaver in the past. However, this has been solved by the inclusion of the innovative Layout view. This is a Design view specifically for creating table formats and it offers a lot more flexibility in terms of design and layout than standard HTML table creation. Complex designs can be created in Layout view and these can then be placed in the Design view, where content can be added.

Content can be added to the table layout in Layout view, as well as in Design view.

Accessing Layout view

To return to Design view from Layout view, click on the Standard View button on the Layout tab on the Insert panel.

| Click on the Layout tab on the Insert panel and click on the Layout View button

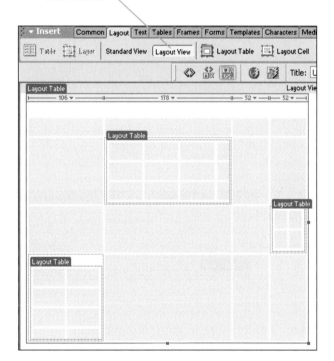

2 The way to tell if you are in Layout view is whether the Layout Table and Layout Cell buttons are active or grayed out. If they are active, you are in Layout view

Creating cells and tables

Tables can be created in Layout view and then have cells added into them, or cells can be drawn directly into Layout view, without first creating a table. If this is done, the table is automatically included to contain the cells. To create tables and cells in Layout view:

Layout view is an excellent way to create asymmetrical table layouts. You can draw cells anywhere you like within a table, and Layout view will automatically format the rest of the table accordingly.

1. Click Layout Table on the Layout tab on the Insert panel to create a new table

2. Click and drag in Layout view to create the border of the table

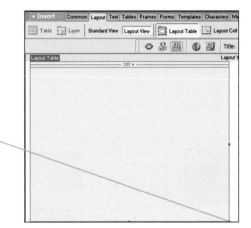

To add multiple cells without having to re-select the Layout Cell button each time, hold down Shift when the Layout Cell button is first selected. Keep it held down while you draw the cells within the table.

3. A tag at the top indicates that it is a table and its width (in pixels) is displayed along the top border of the table

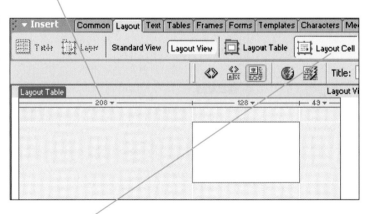

Once the Layout Cell button has been selected, cells can be created in the table by dragging within it.

4. Click here on the Layout tab on the Insert panel to add cells within the table. (This step can be done first, in which case a table will automatically be created to enclose the cells)

...cont'd

Content and borders

If a table is created in Layout view and it has no content or table borders then nothing will be visible when it is viewed in a browser. If a border is added then the cells that have been drawn in Layout view will be visible when viewed in a browser.

Table borders can only be added in Design view. For a table that has been created in Layout view, the borders will appear around the whole table and also the cells that have been created. Although the rest of the table is outlined with a dotted line in Design view, this does not appear in the browser, unless content is added to it. If this is done, then the cell into which the new content has been added it also visible in the browser and it will also now appear in Layout view.

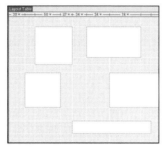

A table in Layout view, with no content or border

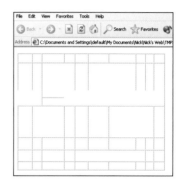

The same table, with a border, viewed in a browser

Formatting

Cells in Layout view can be moved by clicking and dragging and resized by selecting them and dragging the resizing handles, in the same way as images are resized. In addition there is also a Properties Inspector that can be used to set the width of tables and cells in Layout view and also to set the cell spacing and padding and the background color. This is accessible whenever the table is selected in Layout view.

An entire table can be selected in Layout view by clicking once on its outer border. It can then be resized by dragging the resizing handles.

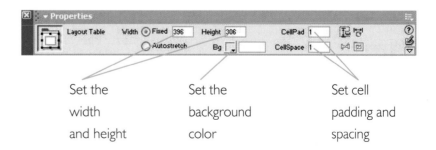

Set the width and height

Set the background color

Set cell padding and spacing

Only one column in a table in Layout view can be set to autostretch. This can be used if you want one part of your page to remain static (perhaps the index column) while the other is stretched to fit the browser window (perhaps the main content of a page).

Even if columns are set to a fixed width, they will expand if content is added larger than the column width.

Spacer images are tiny transparent images that Layout view inserts to make autostretch work properly. They are needed to make the column think that there is content in it, even though it is invisible. Spacer images are important because cells without any content would collapse.

An autostretch column in Layout view is denoted by a wavy line at the top. Any table column can be allotted as autostretch. This means it will resize to enable the whole table to fit the browser window.

Column width

One of the traditional problems with tables is that the designer does not always know how they will appear in different browsers. Layout view attempts to overcome this by enabling different parts of a table to be given different attributes as far as its width is concerned. The options are either to have a fixed width, which remains the same in every browser, or have an autostretch width. This means that a column with autostretch will expand to fit the remainder of the browser window. By default, all columns are a fixed width. To create autostretch columns:

1 Click here and select Make Column Autostretch

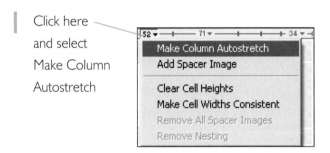

2 Select Create a spacer image file, when prompted. Click OK

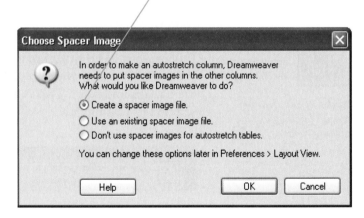

3 Save the spacer image into your website folder

4 The column is now stretched so that the table fills the whole screen

Frames and layers

Two of the more complex elements of Web authoring are frames and layers. Frames enable different files to be viewed simultaneously and layers enable elements on a page to be placed on top of one another. This chapter looks at creating pages using frames and targeting links that are placed in frames pages. It also shows how to create and manage layers.

Covers

Chapter Nine

About frames

Traditionally frames have had an uneasy relationship with the Web, primarily for two reasons:

Frames layouts are frequently used to display an index on the page, which remains there while the rest of the content on screen changes. This way, the user always has quick access to the other main areas on the site. A similar effect can also be achieved through the use of navigation bars.

- They can cause problems for people viewing pages with older browsers such as before Internet Explorer 3 and Netscape Navigator 3, and even when viewed on more recent browsers they are not always displayed as they should be. Also, frames pages can cause problems for search engines when they are trying to catalogue pages

- They are one of the harder concepts for Web designers to master, particularly those new to this medium. Although there is no particular secret to getting to grips with frames from a design point-of-view, there are some elements about them (such as the relationship between frames and framesets and targeting links in frames) that are a bit more confusing than other aspects of Web design

Practise creating and using frames and framesets before you base a website on them. Some people thrive on designing in this way, while others never really take to it.

The basic concept of frames is that the content of two or more pages is displayed on screen at the same time. Each page is known as a frame and numerous frames can be displayed at the same time. Each frame acts independently of the others that are being displayed; so it is possible to scroll through the contents of one frame, while all of the others remain static. This is the great strength of a frames layout: it allows different HTML pages to be viewed simultaneously, without the need to jump from one to another through the use of hyperlinks.

Frames pages are just normal HTML documents. They can be displayed as single pages on their own and they only become part of a frames layout when they are inserted into a frameset.

The final part of the frames equation is the frameset. This is the document that contains all of the frames that are being viewed. So if there are two frames on a page, this involves three documents: the two frames pages and the frameset. The frameset is a separate HTML document that has no visible content of its own. Instead it contains a command for the browser to display the frames that it specifies. It can also contain other details of how to display the frames. Frames pages cannot be displayed in a frames format without a frameset.

Creating frames

Before a frameset can be saved, the individual frames have to be created. This can be done by opening new documents and making them into frames, using preset designs, or using an existing document and adding frames to it. In all cases this is the basis for a frameset, but all of the elements have to be saved before this can be created.

Frames from new documents

Depending on how well you can visualize frames and framesets, it can be easier to build them up from scratch, rather than trying to convert existing documents into this style. However, as you become more familiar with this concept, you may find that both ways are just as easy.

1 Select File>New from the Menu bar

2 Select the General tab and click on Framesets. Select the required design. Click Create

OR

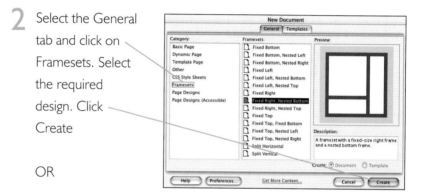

Select Insert>Frames and the required option from the Menu bar

A frameset cannot be used until all of the documents have been saved i.e. all of the files that are going to make up the frames and also the frameset itself, which has to be saved as an individual document.

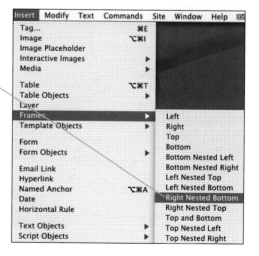

3 Add content for each frame i.e. each file

Using preset designs

1 Click on the Frames tab on the Insert panel

The preset designs can be edited after they have been selected and created on the page.

2 Select a style for your frames layout by clicking on one of these buttons once

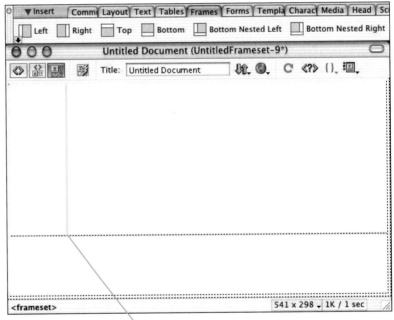

Existing documents can also be inserted directly into a frame structure. To do this, select a frame on screen by clicking on it once. Then select File> Open in Frame and select the document that you want to serve as that particular frame.

3 The selected style opens in the document window

Saving frames and framesets

Once a frames structure has been created and the content for each frame has been added, the frameset can then be created. This consists of saving all of the individual frames documents and then creating a new document that will serve as the frameset. This can be done in two ways:

Think of the frameset as the control file that specifies which files are going to be displayed on the page and how they are going to be formatted.

Saving individual items

Each frame can be saved individually and the frameset can be created at the end. To do this:

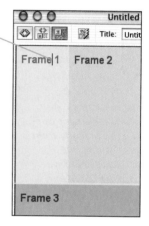

1 Select a frame document by clicking once in its window

2 Select File>Save Frame from the Menu bar and name and save the file as you would with any other HTML document

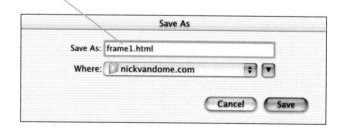

Framesets can be named in the same way as any other HTML document i.e. "accounts.htm". However, in order to identify it as being a frameset document you might want to give it a name such as "acountsframe.htm".

3 Once all of the individual frames files have been saved, select File>Save Frameset from the Menu bar to save the frameset file. Once this has been saved it means that when this file is viewed in a browser it will automatically display the files that have been saved in Step 2

Saving all frames

Once the content
has been added to
all of the frames,
select File>Save All
from the Menu bar

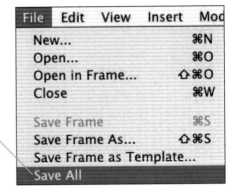

*Use the Save
All command
to save a
frameset and
the files within
it, if you have edited the
content in the frames. Also,
each individual element can
be saved independently from
the others. To save the
frameset, select File>Save
Frameset from the Menu
bar and to save a frame,
insert the cursor in it and
select File>Save from the
Menu bar.*

2 The Save As dialog box will prompt you to save all of the unsaved
frames and the frameset. The frameset is the first one. Give this a
name and click on Save

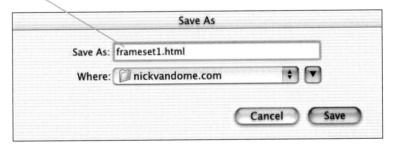

3 Name and save all of the frames in the frameset. The dialog box
for each one will appear automatically after the previous one has
been saved

Frames panel

Sometimes one of the hardest things about frames is to visualize how all of the different elements go together. This is not always obvious when they are being viewed in the document window, particularly at the stage where content has not been added to all of the frames.

Individual frames pages can be edited within the frameset or opened as separate documents and edited. Then, when they are viewed in the frameset, any changes that have been made, such as the background color, will be visible.

To make life easier when dealing with frames, Dreamweaver provides a Frames panel which displays the individual frames within a frameset and also details about the frameset itself. When a frame or frameset is selected in the Frames panel, its details are displayed in the Frames Properties Inspector, which is activated automatically. To view the Frames panel:

1 Open a frameset or create a new one. It does not matter if it contains content or not

2 Select Window>Others>Frames from the Menu bar

When a frame is selected in the Frames panel, it is highlighted in the document window with a thin dotted line around it.

3 The frameset structure and individual frames are displayed. Click in a frame to select it and activate its properties in the Frame Properties Inspector. Click on the outside border to view the frameset properties

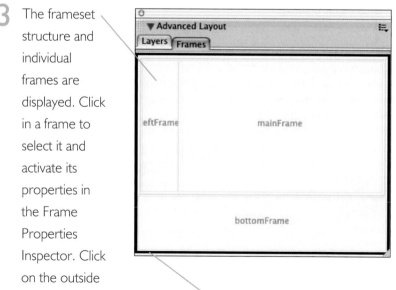

Frame/frameset properties

As with other elements in Dreamweaver, the properties of individual frames and also framesets can be viewed in the Frames Properties Inspector and various settings can be applied.

Frame properties

To view the properties of a frame, it has to be selected, preferably within an open frameset, but it can also be opened as an independent file.

The properties for a frames page that has been opened independently from the frameset can be displayed by clicking once on its outer border in the Frames panel.

If frames have not been given unique names they will be called mainFrame, rightFrame etc. The mainFrame is known as the parent frame in the frameset and the other frames are child frames.
The names of frames become important when it comes to targeting links in frames. For this, they can have unique names that they have been given or their default names.

The Scroll function allows for scroll bars to be inserted if the content in the frame is greater than the available screen size. The default is for using scroll bars and this should only be turned off if you are sure that they will not be needed.

1 Open a frameset, select Window> Others>Frames and click on a frame in the Frames panel

2 Click here to give the frame a unique name

3 Click here to specify whether a frame has a border and, if so, its designated color

4 Click here to specify whether the frame can use scroll bars or not when it is viewed in a browser

5 Check this box on if you do not want users to be able to change the size of the frame when it is viewed in a browser

Frameset properties

A framuset can be given a name by selecting it as shown in step 1 and then selecting Modify> Page Properties. Enter a name in the Title box. This is the one that will appear as the page title, rather than the filename.

1 Open a frameset, select Window> Others>Frames and click on the outer border in the Frame panel

OR

Click on one of the frame borders in the document window

2 The format of the frameset is displayed here

3 Click here to specify whether the frameset uses borders and, if so, a designated color

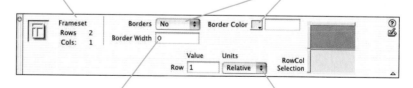

4 If borders are used, click here to specify a weight of line for them

5 Click here to specify the size of a frame, which can be determined by selecting one of the panels to the right

Resizing and deleting frames

Frames can be resized in a frameset or deleted from it altogether.

Resizing a frame

A frame can be resized by selecting the frameset and then resizing it in the Frameset Properties Inspector, but it is probably quicker to resize it by dragging:

Individual frames can also be selected by Alt+click (Windows) or Option+Shift+click (Mac) within the required frames document. This activates the Frames Properties Inspector, as long as the frames document has been selected while it is being viewed within its frameset document.

Make sure the Frames panel is showing by selecting Window>Others>Frames from the Menu bar

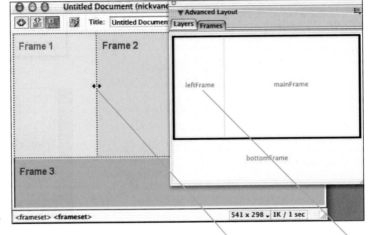

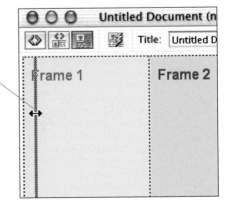

Once a frame has been resized, select the frame and select File>Save from the Menu bar, or File> Save All to save all of the frames and the frameset.

Click on the border of a frame and drag to resize it. The Frames panel will display the frame being resized

Deleting a frame

Click on the border of a frame and drag it to the outer border of the frameset to delete it

Hyperlinks in frames

Since framesets are essentially a collection of standard HTML pages displayed alongside each other, it is safe to assume that they contain exactly the same range of elements as a page being displayed on it own. This can include text, images, tables and, most importantly, hyperlinks. The reason that hyperlinks have a more significant role to play in framesets is because they do not behave exactly in the same way as on a single page. If a hyperlink is on a standard HTML page then the linked page opens in place of the one in which the link was placed. However, since a frameset has a minimum of two frames, this means that there is a choice for where a linked page is displayed. By default a linked page opens in the same frame as the link was placed:

When using hyperlinks in a frameset, bear in mind that the area in which the linked page will be opened will probably be smaller than if it were opened independently in its own window. This could have some consequences for the design and layout of the linked page.

1 In this basic frameset (created with two frames) a hyperlink has been placed in the left-hand frame

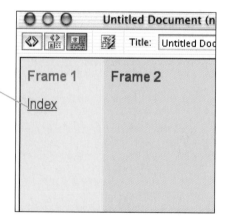

2 When the hyperlink is activated, the linked page opens up in the same frame, unless otherwise specified

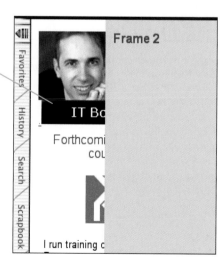

Targeting links

There may be occasions when you will want a linked page to open in the same frame as the one in which the link is placed. However, it is more likely that you will want to specify another frame for the linked file to open in. This is known as targeting links.

The most obvious example of targeting links is in a frameset with one frame acting as an index and the other as the main display area for the content. The links are placed in the index and when they are activated, the linked file is opened in the main frame. This means that the selected content is displayed and the index is still visible. To target a link in a frameset, it has to first be created and then you have to specify the frame in which you want it to open in the frameset:

When adding hyperlinks to a frame, make sure all of the elements of the frameset have been saved.

1 Create a hyperlink in a frame as you would on an independent page

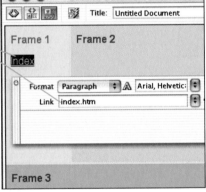

When you first start experimenting with targeting links, use a simple frameset containing two frames at first. This will enable you to get a feel for how targeting works and you can then apply it to more complex framesets. This is one of the more confusing aspects of HTML authoring so take some time to practise with it.

2 Click here in the Properties Inspector to select the options for targeting the link

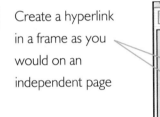

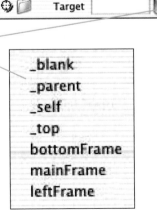

The options for targeting a link are:

Using the "Blank" option for targeting can be confusing or irritating for users, particularly if they are not too experienced with the Web. Having more than one browser window open at the same time can make some users uncertain about which one they should be using.

- Blank. This opens the linked document in a new window and leaves the original frameset intact

- Parent. This opens the linked document in the main frame (or parent) of the frameset

- Self. This opens the linked document in the same frame as the one in which the link is located

- Top. This opens the linked document in the whole frameset, so that none of the previous content is visible

3 Once a link has been targeted, the linked document will open in the specified frame. In this example, the linked document has been targeted to open in the _parent frame, which means it opens in the main frame window

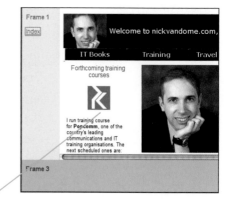

The "Top" option can be useful if you want to take the user to the start of a separate section within your website. This could then open as a complete window and so give more prominence to the items in that section. Also, by removing the other frames, there will be less distractions for the user.

4 If the targeted link had been to _top, the link would have opened as a whole page and the index would not have been visible any more

Targeting with named frames

If you are using a limited number of frames within a frameset (two or three) then it is relatively straightforward to keep track of targeting frames with the _blank, _parent, _self and _top options. However if you are using a frameset containing numerous frames, it can get confusing as to which links are going to appear in which frames.

To overcome this problem, it is possible to use frame names as the targeted links. To do this:

Frames can be named by selecting them and then entering a name for them in the Properties Inspector. See page 140 for details about assigning frame properties.

1 Select frames in the Frames panel and then name them in the Frame Properties Inspector

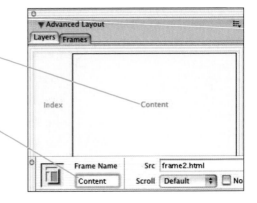

2 Add a link in a frame and click here to access the targeting options

Even if frames have not been named, the target list also contains options for targeting frames such as "mainFrame" or "topFrame" which refer to the active frames and their position in the frameset. However, this can get confusing if there are numerous frames in the frameset.

3 A list of all the named frames within the frameset will appear. Select one and this is where the linked file will be opened

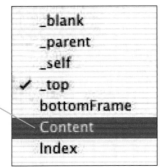

Using layers

One of the drawbacks of Web pages created in HTML is that there has not always been a facility to overlap elements on a page, such as text over an image, or several images stacked on top of each other. However, Dreamweaver has made this possible with a function called layers. This allows layers of content to be added to a page, which can be positioned independently from the items that have already been included: they are placed on an invisible layer above the elements underneath, as if they were included on a piece of glass or transparent plastic.

Layers can give a degree of flexibility that has not previously been available in some Web authoring programs:

Layers are created using the <div> </div> or the <span> </span> HTML tags.

Both Internet Explorer 4 or later and Netscape Navigator 4 or later support the full functionality of layers. Earlier browsers may be able to display them, but not necessarily with the correct positioning.

If a page contains layers, always make sure you preview it in a Web browser before you publish it. This is true for all pages but particularly so for those containing layers, because the positioning can sometimes be different when viewed in a browser. If possible, view the pages with layers in different browsers.

Birthday Cake

Previously with Web authoring programs, it was not always possible to overlap elements on the page

Birthday Cake

In Dreamweaver, the use of layers enables multiple items to be placed on top of each other

Creating layers

A single layer can be added to a page, or numerous ones can be included. Layers have to be inserted before content can be added to them. To do this:

Default layer properties can be specified in the Preferences dialog box by selecting Edit>Preferences from the Menu bar and selecting the Layers category.

1 On the Common tab on the Insert panel, click on the Layer button

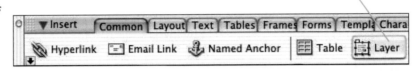

If you hold down Shift when you select the Layer button (on the Insert panel's Common tab) you will be able to draw multiple layers on the page, one after the other, as long as you continue to keep Shift held down.

2 Click and drag in the document window to draw the layer

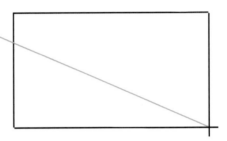

Layers can also be created by selecting Insert>Layer from the Menu bar, or by dragging and dropping the Layer button from the Common panel on the Insert panel.

3 A layer marker will appear at the top left of the page. This is an invisible element and if you cannot see it, select View>Visual Aids>Invisible Elements from the Menu bar

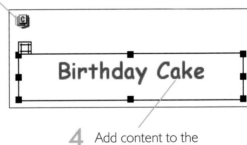

4 Add content to the layer as you would on a standard page

Layer properties

When a layer is selected, its properties are displayed in the Layer Properties Inspector and various settings can be applied to the selected layer. To do this:

Clicking anywhere inside a layer activates it rather than selects it. This means that content can then be added to it.

1 Select a layer by clicking on its border once or by clicking the layer anchor point invisible element. This activates the Layer Properties Inspector

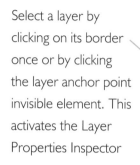

The Layers Properties Inspector also has options for how the content is displayed (Vis) and also for inserting a background or color.

2 Give the layer a meaningful name. This is advisable if you are going to be using a lot of layers

3 Enter values in the L and T boxes to specify the position of the layer from the top left corner. Enter values in the W and H boxes for the layer dimensions

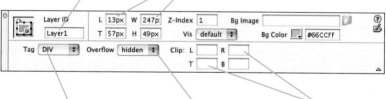

The z-index option in the Properties Inspector can be used to change the stacking order of layers, but this is easier to do through the Layers panel (see overleaf).

4 Click here to select the type of HTML tag that is used for layers

5 Click here to specify how the layer reacts if the content is bigger than it (CSS layers only)

6 Click here to set the visible area of layers, in pixels

Layers panel

The Layers panel can be used to perform certain editing and management tasks with layers. It is particularly effective when there are two or more layers on a page.

Accessing the Layers panel

New layers cannot be created from the Layers panel. This has to be done from the Menu bar (Insert>Layer) or the Layer button on the Common tab on the Insert panel.

1 Select Window>Others>Layers from the Menu bar

2 Click here (Eye symbol) to show or hide the layers in the current document window

If you do not want the content in individual layers to overlap one another, check on the Prevent Overlaps box in the Layers panel. If you then try and drag a layer over another one in the document window, you will not be able to do so.

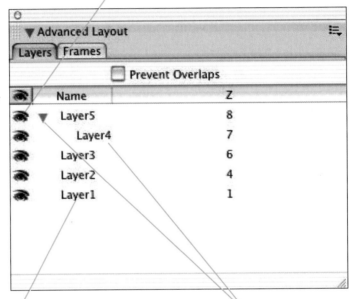

The stacking order of layers (i.e. the order in which they can be placed on top of each other) can be changed in the Layers panel by clicking on a layer and dragging it to the point you want it to appear in the stacking order. The first layer in the Layers panel is the one that is at the top of the stacking order.

3 The earliest created layer is at the bottom of the list. Any new layers will be added at the top of the list

4 Nested layers (i.e. those created or placed inside another layer) are shown as being attached to the layer in which they are nested. Click on the arrow to expand or contract the nested structure

Creating nested layers

One of the most versatile features of layers is their ability to be nested inside each other. This can allow for several elements to be stacked together while remaining in the same overall layer. To create nested layers:

1 Create a layer in Design view

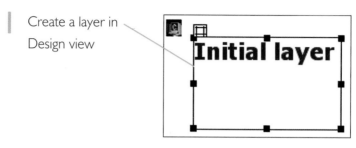

2 Drag the Layer button from the Common tab on the Insert panel and drop it into the existing layer

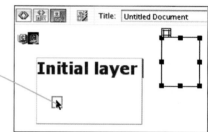

 Nested layers can also be created in the Layers panel by holding down Ctrl (Windows) or Command (Mac) then clicking on and dragging a layer until it is positioned over the layer in which you want to nest it. Release the mouse button to create a nested layer.

3 Alternatively, select the Layer button by clicking on it once and draw a layer to the required size within the existing layer

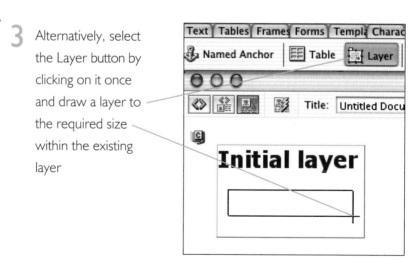

4 Alternatively, insert the cursor in the existing layer and select Insert>Layer from the Menu bar

Moving and resizing layers

Layers can be moved and resized in a similar way to working with images:

Moving layers

If you insert content into a layer that is larger than the dimensions of the layer, it will expand automatically to accommodate the content.

1 Select a layer by clicking once on its border

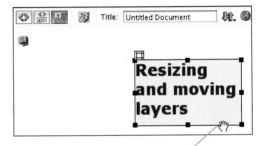

If you think your layers page will be viewed in browsers that will not support layers (Internet Explorer 3 or earlier or Netscape 3 or earlier) then you can convert layers content into a table. To do this, select the layer, then select Modify>Convert> Layers to Table from the Menu bar. Select OK in the next dialog box. This will only work if there are no nested or overlapping layers.

2 Click and drag on one of the borders of the layer (but not one of the black square resizing handles) and move the layer to the required location. Any content in the layer moves with it

Resizing layers

1 Select a layer by clicking once on its border

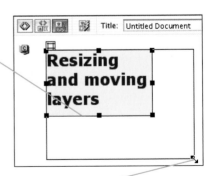

2 Click and drag the resizing handles to increase or decrease the size of the layer (a layer cannot be made smaller than the size of the largest object in it)

Advanced features

As well as its standard Web authoring features, Dreamweaver also has a range of some of the most powerful Web design tools available, including Cascading Style Sheets, animations, Flash effects, Javascript and features for creating dynamic Web pages. This chapter looks at some of these features and shows how they can be used to create high quality, professional sites.

Covers

Chapter Ten

Forms

A HTML form is a set of objects that the user can interact with to send various pieces of information to the server hosting the Web page, or directly to the author of the page, which require a piece of computer programming called a script. This can collate the information from the form, analyze it and send it to a specified location. This can be done with a variety of scripting languages, such as Perl or Javascript. The script can either be placed within the form itself (client-side) or on the server that will be processing the information (server-side). If it is a server-side application, this is usually handled with a Common Gateway Interface script.

A form can be made up of several different elements, all of which are contained in an overall form container. Attributes and properties can then be assigned to each element within the form structure. To create a form and set its properties:

If your website containing forms is going to be published by your Internet Service Provider (ISP), check with them first to make sure that they can process forms and also for any special requirements they need included in the form.

Common Gateway Interface (CGI) scripts are usually written in computer languages such as Perl, C or Java. This is not something that can be picked up in a couple of days but if you really want to get into it, perhaps the best place to start is to get a copy of Perl in easy steps.
There are also a number of sites on the Web that offer information about CGIs, including some scripts that can be downloaded and used. One site to look at is `http://www.cgi-resources.com/`

2 Click the Form button to add the form container

1 Click the Forms tab on the Insert panel

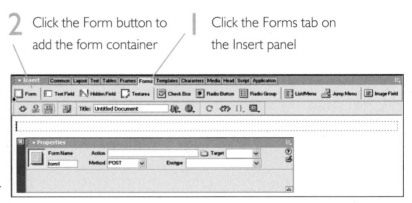

The properties for a form are entered in the Form Properties Inspector and they are:

- Form Name. This is a unique identifier for the form

- Action. If the form is being processed by a server-side script enter the URL of the script here

- Method. This is the way information is sent to the server. The options are Get, Post and Default

- Enctype. The type of encryption used if the form requires to be secure i.e. if it deals with financial transactions

Form elements

There are a variety of elements that can be added to forms and these are accessed from the Forms tab on the Insert panel. The available options are:

A form has a non-printing border that can be used to help format items within the form. If this is not visible when the form is inserted, select View>Visual Aids>Invisible Elements from the Menu bar.

- Text Field. This can be used to insert single lines of data, multiple lines of data or passwords

- Hidden Field. This can be inserted into a form to capture information about the user, or the form itself

- Textarea. Similar to a text field except that it contains scroll bars so that unlimited text can be entered

- Check Box. This can be used with a list of options that the user has to select as required. In a list of check boxes, numerous items can be selected: it is not an either/or option

- Radio Button. Similar to check boxes, except that they only allow for a single option to be selected

Forms take on the background color of the page on which they are created. However, text and images can be formatted independently within a form. Tables can also be inserted within a form and the form elements placed inside them for formatting purposes.

- Radio Group. This allows for groups of radio buttons to be inserted, with each group containing a different option

- List/Menu. Creates a drop-down list or menu

- Jump Menu. Creates a drop-down menu with items that contain a hyperlink to another page or object

- Image Field. This can be used to insert an image into a form, generally for design purposes

- File Field. This allows the user to select a file from their hard drive and insert it into the form

- Button. This can be used to insert Submit or Reset buttons

- Label. This is an optional button that can be used to give textual labels to form elements

- Fieldset. This is a container for a group of related form elements

Cascading Style Sheets styles

Cascading Style Sheets (CSS) styles are similar in some ways to HTML styles in that they are a collection of formatting attributes that can be applied to items of text or whole documents. However, they have much greater flexibility because they can also control non-textual attributes such as positioning and list formatting. CSS styles can be linked to numerous files within a Web structure and when one CSS style is updated all of the affected items throughout the site are updated as well.

CSS styles are only fully supported by browser versions 4.0 and above of Internet Explorer and Netscape Navigator. Earlier versions may support some CSS styles, but it is unlikely that they will support all of them.

It is possible to link a file to an existing CSS style that has already been created, or you can create your own CSS styles within a Dreamweaver document. There are three types of CSS styles that can be created within Dreamweaver:

An external CSS style sheet is a text file containing formatting attributes. It is possible to link to these and use the formatting styles with your own documents.

- Make Custom Style. This can be used to create a CSS style that can be applied to selected items throughout a document, or several documents

- Redefine HTML Tag. This can be used to change the attributes of an existing HTML tag, such as a heading or a hyperlink. Once this CSS style has been defined, all of the affected elements will be changed automatically, they do not have to be selected within the documents

- Use CSS Selector. This can be used to change the attributes for specific elements within a CSS style. For instance, if you want to change the color of a hyperlink when the cursor is placed over it, but no other attributes of it, then Use CSS Selector can be used to edit this particular item

The code for CSS styles is placed in the head tag of a HTML page. For the Make Custom Style option, a tag is also placed around the selected text, to show that the CSS style should only be applied to this element. Once you have created a CSS style, click on the HTML Source button on the Launcher to see where the code for the CSS style has been inserted.

Creating CSS styles

To create CSS styles that can be applied to documents in Dreamweaver:

1 Click on the CSS Styles panel

2 Click the arrow and select New CSS Style in the menu or click on the New CSS Style button

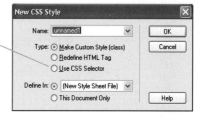

Custom CSS styles are identified by the <class> tag in the HTML source code.

3 Name the style and allocate a type here

When giving a name to a custom CSS style, it has to start with a full stop, followed by an alphabetical character. There should not be any spaces in the name. This will identify it as a "–.class" file.

4 Or click Redefine HTML Tag to alter the attributes for an existing HTML tag and select the tag here

5 Or click Use CSS Selector and select a particular attribute here

6 Click OK to access the properties for all of the above

7 Select the attributes for the CSS style you want to create. This is done in the CSS Style definition for... dialog box, which contains eight categories

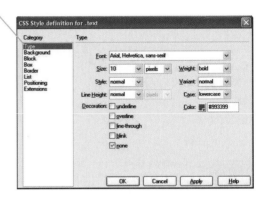

The Decoration options in the Type category can be used to display hyperlinks in a format other than the standard underlined one. Check on the "None" box under Decoration and then when this is applied to a link, it will appear without underlining.

The categories for setting the attributes for a CSS style are:

- Type. This contains font formatting attributes and also attributes that can be applied to hyperlinks

- Background. This contains attributes for background colors and images and determines whether the background is static or moves when the page scrolls

- Block. This contains attributes for aligning text and specifying how much space is placed around text

CSS style formatting can be overridden by manual formatting and, in some cases, by HTML styles. If you are using CSS styles, make sure that all manual formatting and HTML styles have been removed.

- Box. This contains attributes that can be applied to elements such as layers that are included in a CSS style. This enables you to position elements with the CSS style

- Border. This contains attributes for borders around items such as tables and images

- List. This contains attributes for formatting lists

- Positioning. This contains attributes for positioning layers

- Extensions. This contains miscellaneous attributes that are not supported by all browsers, so they are best left alone

Applying CSS styles

When CSS styles are created for Redefine HTML Tags and Use CSS Selector these are automatically placed into the head tag of the document and apply to the entire file. So, if the attributes for the H1 tag have been changed, this will alter the formatting for all of the occurrences of this tag in the document. However, with custom CSS styles, specific text has to be selected to have the style applied to it. To do this:

If a custom CSS style is edited, all of the items that have had its attributes applied to them will automatically be updated.

1 Create a Make Custom style in the CSS Styles panel and give it a name

2 Select the text to which you want to apply the style

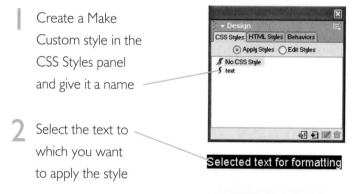

Selected text for formatting

3 Apply the style by clicking on it once in the CSS Styles panel

Different CSS styles can be applied within the same piece of text. To do this, select a piece of text and apply a CSS style to it. Then select a smaller piece of text within the main selection and apply another style. As long as there is no conflict between the styles they will both be applied to the smaller selection.

selected text for formatting

4 The file includes details of the CSS in the HTML source code head

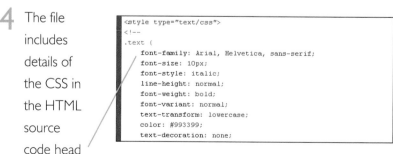

```
<style type="text/css">
<!--
.text {
    font-family: Arial, Helvetica, sans-serif;
    font-size: 10px;
    font-style: italic;
    line-height: normal;
    font-weight: bold;
    font-variant: normal;
    text-transform: lowercase;
    color: #993399;
    text-decoration: none;
```

Animation

Although Dreamweaver does not have the power and versatility of a program like Flash for creating animated elements for the Web, it does offer some basic techniques for animating text and images.

Animations in Dreamweaver use the standard technique of placing an object on a timeline and then moving it between various points. The timeline is a series of frames (like the frames that make up a film or video) and you can specify what object appears in a certain frame and its position. Objects can then be manipulated in the timeline to alter elements such as their speed. In Dreamweaver, objects have to be placed in a layer before they can be inserted into a timeline to animate them. (For more on layers, see Chapter Nine). Several objects can be animated at the same time, as long as they are all placed in separate layers. To animate an object:

Flash, also from Macromedia, is the definitive program for creating Web animations. For a free 30-day trial, look on Macromedia's website at `www.macromedia.com/` `software/flash/` `download.`

For a detailed look at Flash, take a look at "Flash MX in easy steps".

1 Create a layer in an open document and insert an object (text or an image). Select the layer by clicking once on its border

The Timeline Inspector has a frame rate for animated objects. This is measured in frames per second (fps) and a good setting for use on a Web page is between 12–15 fps.

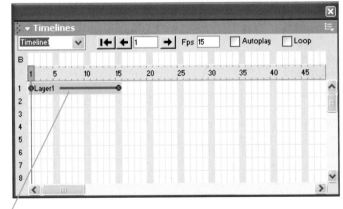

2 To place the object on the animation timeline, select Modify> Timeline>Add Object to Timeline from the Menu bar

3   In the Timeline Inspector the object is positioned at frame 1 i.e. the beginning of its animation path

The bulleted dots that appear in the timeline are known as keyframes. These indicate a point where an object is positioned in a new location. When creating an animation in Dreamweaver you specify the initial position of an object in the first keyframe, select the next keyframe by clicking on it once, and then move the position of the object. Dreamweaver then creates the animation between these two points.

5   Move the object on the page. A line should appear – this is the path the animation will take

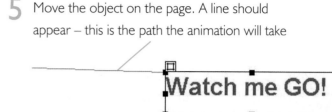

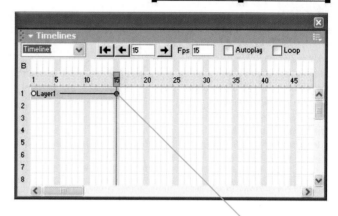

4   Click on the marker at the end of the timeline

The length of an animation can be shortened or lengthened by clicking on the second keyframe and dragging it along the timeline.

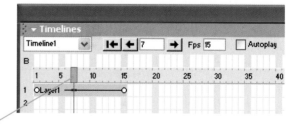

6   Drag the red marker (the Playhead) to and fro to see how the object animates

Modifying animation paths

In addition to creating straight line animations, it is also possible to create them with a curved or freeform path.

Creating a curved path

1 Create a straight-line animation, as on the previous page

Several items can be animated at the same time by creating them on different layers within the Timeline panel (this is not the same as the layer in the document window). To do this, click on the row in the Timeline panel below the current animation then insert a layer and add a new object. Make sure the layer is selected, then select Modify>Timeline>Add Object to Timeline and then animate it in the same way as on pages 160–161.

2 Right click (Windows) or Ctrl+click (Mac) at a point between the two keyframes and select Add Keyframe from the contextual menu

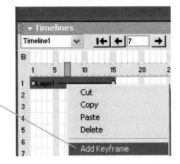

3 Move the object to create a curved path for the animation

Creating a freeform path

1 Create a layer with content and select Modify>Timeline>Record Path of Layer from the Menu bar

2 Click and drag the layer to create as simple or complex a path as required. This is the path the animation will follow

Flash buttons and text

Flash is an animation program that has become the industry standard for producing animated effects on the Web. As with Dreamweaver, it is also produced by Macromedia and in Dreamweaver MX some of the power of Flash has been harnessed through the use of animated buttons and text. This allows Web designers in Dreamweaver to create buttons and text that change appearance when the user moves the cursor over them. To create Flash buttons or text (the process is almost exactly the same for both; this example is for a button):

1 Select Flash Button (or Flash Text) on the Media tab on the Insert panel

2 Select a pre-designed style for the button

3 Add the text you want to appear on the button

4 Enter a hyperlink for the button

5 Click OK

6 Select the button and click Play to view the effect when the cursor is passed over it

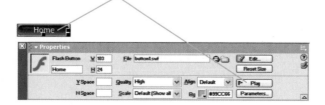

Behaviors

Behaviors in Dreamweaver are preprogrammed events that are triggered by the user performing a certain action on the page. For instance, the action of rolling the cursor over an image could trigger the event of a sound being played. Behaviors are created by Javascript programming but Dreamweaver contains several pre-written behaviors that can be inserted into a page using the Behaviors Inspector.

Creating a behavior consists of two parts, defining the action that is going to be performed and stating the event that will be triggered by the action. There are several events that can be selected and more can be downloaded from the Web. When an event is selected the action to trigger it is automatically included. To create a behavior:

All browsers handle behaviors differently. In the Behaviors panel it is possible to specify the version of the browser for which you are creating the behavior.

If you want to attach a behavior to a whole page, create it without selecting anything within the document. This behavior is usually triggered when the document is opened on the Web, and is identified by the onLoad event.

Select an item to which you want to attach a behavior, such as an image

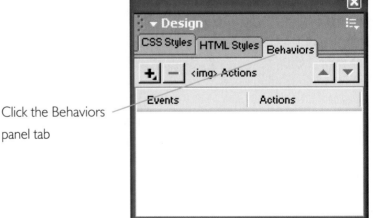

2 Click the Behaviors panel tab

The script for behaviors is inserted into the head portion of the HTML source code. If you know Javascript you can write your own scripts and include them as behaviors.

3 Click here to access the Actions menu. Select the action that you want to use for the selected item

4 The action is entered and the default event (the one that will trigger the action) is inserted. Here it is 'onMouseOver' which means the action will be triggered when the cursor is rolled over the selected item

The events associated with selected images, text or hyperlinks include:

- *onMouseOver, which is when the cursor is moved over the selected item*
- *onMouseOut, which is when the cursor is moved off the selected item*
- *onClick, which is when the selected item is clicked on*

5 Click here to access alternative options for the default event, if any are available

onMouseDown

onMouseMove

onMouseOut

onMouseOver

onMouseUp

Javascript

In Dreamweaver, some effects, such as rollover buttons, are created using a programming language called Javascript. This is a popular language for use on the Web and it can be inserted into Web pages for a variety of uses, such as producing scrolling text or dates that update themselves automatically. If you are proficient in writing Javascript, it is possible to write and insert this code yourself. (It is also possible to include other scripting languages such as VBScript). To insert Javascript into a Dreamweaver page:

Scripts can be entered while you are working in Design view or Code view, or a combination of both.

1 Click the Script button on the Script tab on the Insert panel

2 Click here to select the type of script to write

To learn Javascript, look at "Javascript in easy steps".

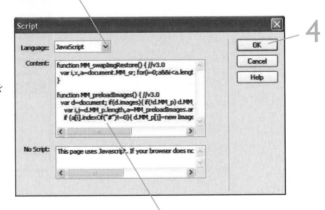

4 Click OK to insert the script into a Dreamweaver file

3 In the Content box, enter your script

For an in-depth look at Javascript and Dreamweaver, select Help> Using Dreamweaver from the Menu bar and select Javascript from the Index.

5 On the toolbar, click here to debug your script in a browser

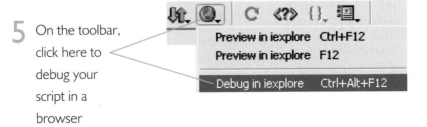

Dynamic Web pages

The server technologies supported by Dreamweaver MX are ColdFusion, ASP, ASP .NET, JSP, and PHP. This means that you can create dynamic content with these languages and Dreamweaver will be able to display the results, as long as you have a Web server (see the tip below).

One of the most important development with Web pages in recent years is dynamic Web pages. These are websites and pages that interact with databases and the pages displayed change depending on the database or the information requested by the users. Dynamic Web pages can be created with server technologies including programming languages such as ColdFusion, Javascript and Active Server Pages (ASP). Dreamweaver MX provides comprehensive support for these technologies to enable developers to work more easily with dynamic pages.

In order to create dynamic Web pages you will require a good understanding of the relevant server technology. However, Dreamweaver MX makes it as painless as possible to produce the initial structure. To do this for dynamic pages:

In order to create and test dynamic Web pages you will need to have a Web server installed on your computer. This is a program that interprets the dynamic content and serves the results to a browser.

Different server technologies use different Web servers but some of them are interchangeable. Three types of Web server are the Personal Web Server, the Internet Information Server (both from Microsoft) and Apache. The Web server is used as the Testing Server in Dreamweaver MX.

1 Select the Server Behaviors panel and click here to create a new dynamic site

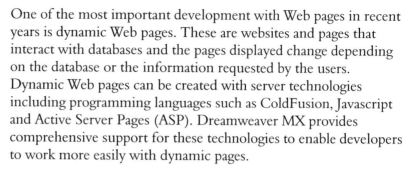

2 Enter a name for the site and select a Local Root Folder

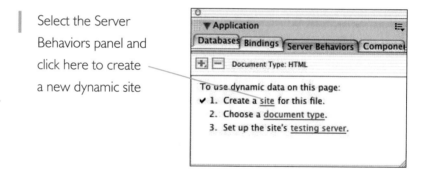

3 Click OK

4 Click here to select the type of dynamic Web language used for your site

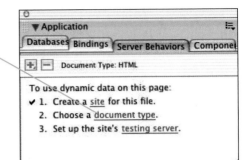

In addition to a Web server you will also require an application server to create dynamic pages. This is software that helps the Web server interpret pages created in a particular dynamic language. Some Web applications include ColdFusion MX and JRun (both from Macromedia), IBM WebSphere and Jakata Tomcat.

5 Click here and select a document type here

Choose Document Type

Choose the Testing Server related Document Type for the current document:

ASP JavaScript

NOTE: Changing the Document Type may change the file extension of your document.

OK

Cancel

Help

✓ ASP JavaScript
ASP VBScript
ASP.NET C#
ASP.NET VB
ColdFusion
ColdFusion Component
JSP
PHP

6 Click OK

Mac OS X has the Apache Web server already installed so you do not have to worry about loading a different Web server. This is automatically used as the Testing Server when a dynamic site is being defined.

7 Click here to select a testing server i.e. a Web server on your computer that can interpret the dynamic pages being used

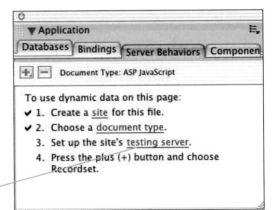

The Web application ColdFusion MX is closely integrated with Dreamweaver MX and is part of the Studio MX package from Macromedia. However, you will still require a Web server once you are using ColdFusion MX to create dynamic content (unless you are using the pre-installed Apache server with Mac OS X.)

8 Select the Testing Server category and select a folder which will act as the testing environment. Click OK

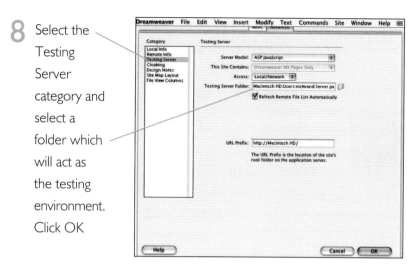

9 Click here and select Recordset (Query) from the menu

The HTML Tag Libraries in Dreamweaver MX contain commonly used tags for all of the server technologies that can be used to create dynamic content i.e. ColdFusion, ASP, ASP .NET, JSP and PHP.

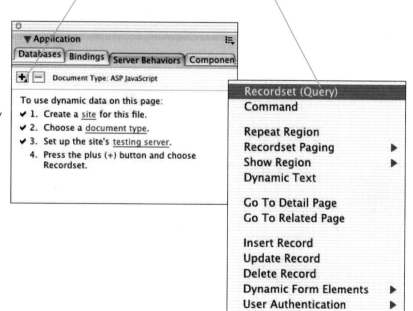

10 At this point, a knowledge of the selected dynamic language is required and also an understanding of working with databases, as these are the foundations of most dynamic Web pages. In the Recordset dialog box, details of databases and their parameters can be set in relation to the dynamic language that is being used:

Once a site has been defined for dynamic Web pages, the Insert panel includes tabs for adding content for the selected server technology. For instance, if ColdFusion is the selected technology then there will be tabs on the Insert panel that allow for ColdFusion elements to be included within the dynamic pages. These can be inserted in a similar way to inserting static elements into a HTML page, but some knowledge of the server technology is required.

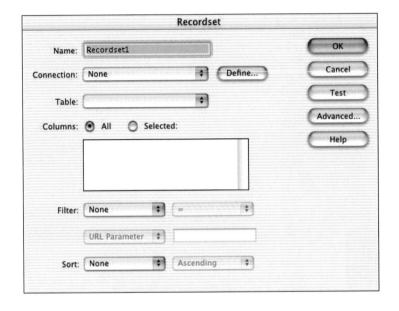

Dynamic Web pages are not for the novice and you will have to have a good understanding of your chosen server technology and also the workings of databases before you start creating dynamic content in Dreamweaver MX.

11 Once a database has been linked to the current site, it can be accessed and edited through the Databases panel

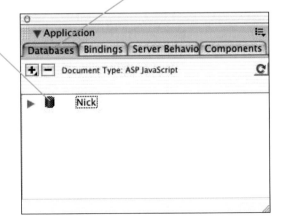

XML

XML is a lot more complicated to use than HTML. For a comprehensive look at this subject have a look at the websites www.xml.com *and* www.w3.org/xml.

Another major recent development in Web page design is the emergence of XML (Extensible Markup Language). Although this is similar in some ways to HTML it enables you to create your own custom tags and produce pages that can interact effectively with databases and convert the information so that it can be viewed in a HTML document. XML is usually used in conjunction with HTML to produce documents known as XHTML. XML is a stricter language than HTML and if it is not written accurately it will not work. Like dynamic Web pages, it is a fairly complex subject but Dreamweaver provides the means to get started:

For a detailed look at XML, take a look at "XML in easy steps".

1. Select File>New from the Menu bar. Select XML under Basic Page and click Create. This creates the start of a XML page

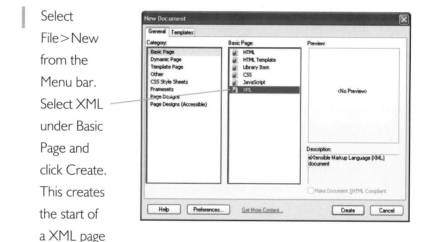

In XML most elements have opening and closing tags, as with HTML. However, if an element does not have a closing tag (usually an element that does not have any textual output) it has to be closed with the forward slash symbol and a closing bracket: />. So a tag for an image could look like this:

<image="nick1.jpg"/>

2. Create the XML content. None of the graphical authoring tools are available in this environment

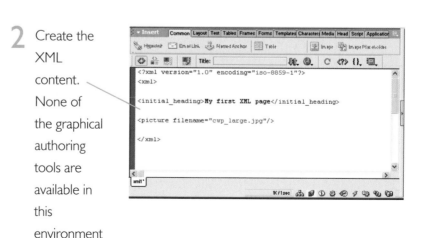

Applying CSS styles to XML documents

CSS styles are a common way of formatting XML documents. Styles can be created that correspond to the custom tags created in the XML document. To do this:

A lot of XML documents are controlled by XML Schemas. These are separate XML documents that define how the output for XML documents will appear. Schemas can be used instead of CSS styles for specifying the final appearance of a XML document.

1 Select File>New from the Menu bar. Select CSS under Basic Page and click Create

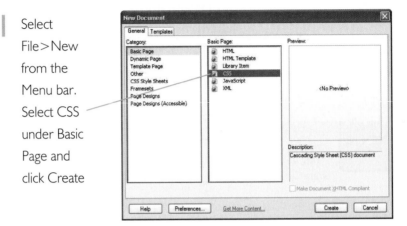

2 Create a CSS file, using style names that correspond to the XML tags

The initial content in a XML document is known as the declaration, which defines the version of XML being used.

3 In the XML document, enter a link to the relevant CSS file

Publishing

This chapter shows some of the checks that can be made before a website is published on the Internet or on an internal network. It also explains the publishing process itself and shows how to work with files once a site has been published.

Covers

Chapter Eleven

Site window preferences

When you have finished designing your website, you can start thinking about uploading your work onto the Web, for the world to see. This involves copying all of the files from your local website, stored on your computer, to a remote site, held on a server that is linked to the Web. This is usually done by a process called File Transfer Protocol (FTP) which is a protocol that enables files to be downloaded from one computer to another. Before this process takes place there are some preferences that can be set and also some site management tasks that can be undertaken. The FTP preferences apply to the site window and they can be set as follows:

If you are working on an intranet site, which operates on an internal network, then your IT systems administrator will be able to give you advice about how to upload your site to the network server.

1 Select Edit>Preferences from the Menu bar

4 Select how shared files are handled

3 Click here to set the location of the local and remote files in the site window

2 In the Preferences dialog box, select the Site category

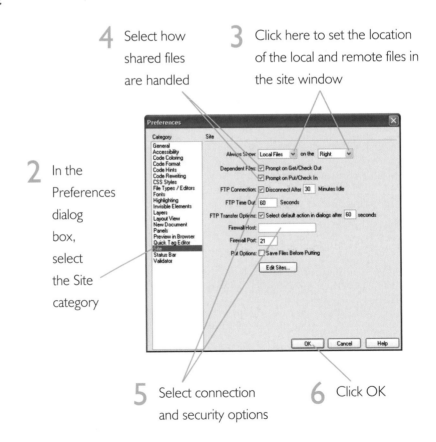

5 Select connection and security options

6 Click OK

Site management

The final step before publishing a site is to check it thoroughly to make sure that everything is working properly. This involves making sure all of the links work and that everything looks the way it should. One way to do this is to preview the site in a browser and go through all of the pages. This can be done by pressing F12 or selecting File>Preview in Browser. Another option is to check all of the hyperlinks in the site window. This will generate a list of all of the broken links in your site and you can then take remedial action. To check the links in your entire site:

The Check Links Sitewide command also reveals files that are orphaned, i.e. ones which do not have any links going to them from other pages. This means that they will not be able to be accessed from anywhere else on the site. It also shows external links, i.e. ones that link to files outside the current site structure.

1 In the Site panel, select the site that you want to check by clicking here

2 Select Site>Check Links Sitewide from the Site panel Menu bar

Broken links occur when the destination address of a hyperlink is changed. This can be for several reasons, such as the file's location has been changed within the site structure or the filename has been changed. If you rename or move files, try and update the relevant hyperlinks at the same time.

3 If there are any broken links in your site they will be listed in the Link Checker panel

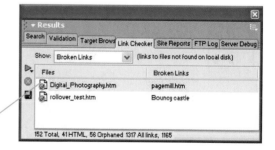

4 To mend a broken link, click on its URL and type in the correct address, or open the relevant file in the document window and select the broken link and add a new link

Using the site map

The site map provides a graphical representation of a site and it can be used to perform various management tasks before the site is published.

Checking the structure

Use the site map to check the overall structure of a site. This can also be used to display broken links within a site:

1. In the Site panel, click here to expand the panel

2. Click here to access the site map

To open a page directly from the site window, double-click on it. It will then be opened in Design view and it can be edited there.

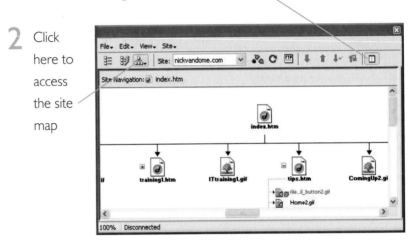

3. The top two levels of the site are displayed. Click on a plus sign to see the linked files below the second level

Checking in and out of files is a function that is used when more than one person is working on the same website. It lets everyone know who is working on a specific file. For more information on this, see page 184.

Within the site map the following symbols and notation are used:

- Red text, or a broken chain link icon, represents a broken hyperlink on the site

- Blue text with a globe icon indicates a link to a file outside the current site structure or an item such as an email link

- Green and red ticks represent files that are checked in or out

- A padlock icon represents files that are read-only (Windows) or locked (Mac)

Formatting the site map

The appearance of the site map can be customized to suit your own preferences:

1 Select Site>Edit Sites from the Menu bar

You can add new files to a site from within the site map and link them directly to existing files. To do this, click once on a file in the site map. Select Site>Link to New File (Windows) or Site>Site Map View>Link to New File (Mac) from the Site panel Menu bar. In the Link to New File dialog box enter a filename for the new file, a page title and the text that will act as a link in the current file to the new one. Select OK and the new file will be inserted in the site map.

Double-click on the initially selected file to open it and view the link to the new file.

2 Select the required site and click Edit

3 In the Site Definition dialog box, click on the Site Map Layout category

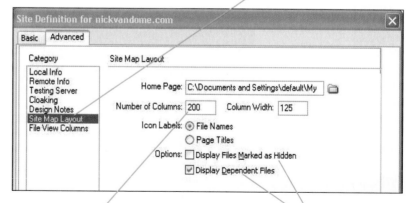

4 Enter values for how the columns of information are displayed

5 Under Icon Labels, set whether files are displayed by page title or file name

6 Specify whether hidden or dependent files are displayed

Uploading a site

Once you have checked your site structure and made sure that there are no broken links on a site, it is time to upload it on to the server that is going to be hosting the site. If you are working on an internal intranet, then the server will probably be part of your local network and the IT systems administrator will be able to advise you about the procedure for uploading a website. If your site is being hosted on the Internet by your Internet Service Provider (ISP), you will require to obtain from them the relevant settings needed when a website is being uploaded.

The process of uploading, or publishing, a website in Dreamweaver consists of creating an exact copy of all of the items within your local site structure, on the remote server. This includes all of the HTML files, images and any other elements that have been included in your site. The same site structure is also retained, so that all of the links in your site will have the same location as their target destination and so work properly.

To upload a site

A lot of ISPs have online advice about uploading your own website and the settings that will be required. Try looking under their Help or Technical Support links. If possible, try to avoid telephoning, since a lot of ISPs charge premium rates for calls to their helplines. Emailing could be a useful compromise if you do not want to telephone.

The local and remote structures may not always be displayed exactly the same as each other when they are uploaded, but the structures will be the same.

When you upload a site to a FTP server, the ISP hosting the site will assign it a Web address (URL). This will probably be based on your own username.

Select Site > Edit Sites from the Menu bar

2 In the Edit Sites dialog box, select a site and select Edit

The Local/ Network settings are much more straightforward than the FTP ones. Since the site will be displayed over an internal network it is just a case of specifying the directory and folder in which you want the site stored.

You will have to get the exact FTP settings from the ISP that is going to be hosting your site. In general terms the details that are needed are:

- *FTP Host. This is the name for identifying the host computer system on the Internet. It is not the same as a Web address (URL) or an email address*

- *Host Directory. This is the location on the host's server where your site will be stored*

- *Login. This is the login name you will use to access your site's files*

- *Password. This is the password that you will use to access your site's files*

Within the FTP settings there are also options for firewalls. This is a security element and you should check with your ISP first before you use these.

3 In the Advanced Site Definition dialog box, select the Remote Info category

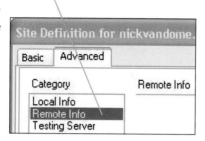

4 Click on Access and select FTP if the site is going to be published on the Web, or Local/Network if it is going to be published on an internal network

5 In the Remote Info section of the Site Definition... dialog box enter details for the FTP Host, the Host Directory, the Login and the Password. (Not all ISPs require Host Directory data, as this is assigned automatically.) When this has been done, click OK (currently hidden) in the dialog box

The Connect button is grayed out, i.e. not available, if the FTP settings have not been entered. However, when it becomes available this is no guarantee that the FTP settings have been entered correctly.

6 In the Edit Sites dialog box, click Done

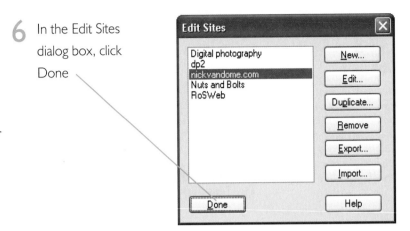

If you have a lot of images in your site structure, or a few large ones, then your site will take longer to upload to the FTP server than if they were not there. This will give you some idea of how long the user will have to wait for certain items to download when they are viewing your site.

7 In the Site panel, click the Connect button. This will connect you to your ISP or local network

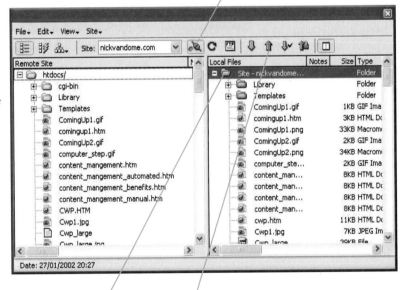

If you experience problems when you try and upload a site with FTP, select View> Site FTP Log from the Site panel Menu bar. This may give you some indication of the problem.

8 Select the root folder and click the Put button. If the site has been uploaded successfully, the Remote folder should be visible in the Site panel and contain a mirror image of the local site

Getting and putting files

If you want to edit a file on your site you can either do so by opening it in the document window and then uploading it to the remote site once the changes have been made, or you can open it from the remote site itself and then make the changes. This involves using the Put and Get commands: Put transfers files from the local folder to the remote server and Get does the reverse:

Putting files

If a file has been edited and updated, the Put command can be used to place it on the remote server:

As with most publishing operations, you require a modem and a current Internet connection to be able to perform the Put and Get actions, if you are connecting to a remote server rather than a local network.

1 In the Site panel, select the file in the local folder by clicking on it once

2 Click the Put button. Dreamweaver will connect to the remote network and place the file in the remote folder

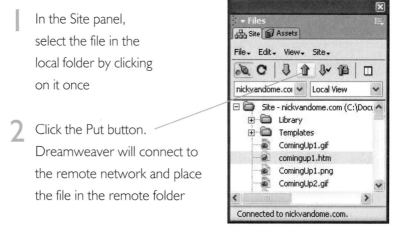

Getting files

1 In the Site panel click here to expand the panel

Once a connection has been made to the remote server, the Connect button changes into a Disconnect one. This indicates that you are online and connected to the remote server. To close the connection, click on the Disconnect button. This will disconnect you from the FTP server but not necessarily your ISP connection. This will probably have to be closed down in the usual way.

2 Select a remote file

3 Click the Get button

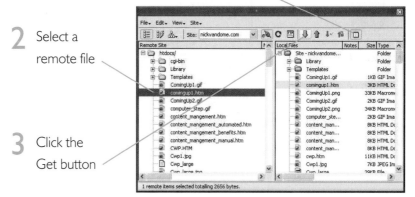

Cloaking

Cloaking is a publishing device that can be used to prevent certain folders or file types being published. This can be useful if you are working on some draft pages or if you want to exclude certain large file types from being published every time you update a site. To use cloaking:

If you want to cloak specific files you have to do this by cloaking the file type in the Site Definition dialog box. This could cause problems if, for instance, you wanted to cloak a HTML file, as all of the other HTML files in the site would also be cloaked. If you do want to cloak specific files, place them in a new folder and apply cloaking to the folder.

1 Select Site>Edit Sites from the Menu bar

2 In the Edit Sites dialog box select a site and click Edit

If you want to specify more than one file type to be cloaked, separate the different types with a single space in the Cloak Files Ending With: box. Do not use a comma or a semicolon.

3 Select the Advanced tab and the Cloaking category

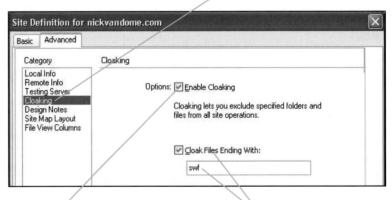

Cloaked items are excluded from site management tasks such as Synchronizing and updating templates and Library items. However, these functions can still be performed by selecting the folder or file individually, as this overrides any cloaking commands.

4 Check on the Enable Cloaking box

5 Check on the Cloak Files Ending With: box and enter any required file types

6 Click OK at the bottom of the dialog box

Applying cloaking

Cloaking can be applied to folders but not individual files (these have to be cloaked by applying a file type to be cloaked in the Site Definition dialog box, as shown on the previous page). To cloak folders:

If you are developing draft sites, make sure they are cloaked when you are publishing other files and folders.

1 Select a folder in the Site panel

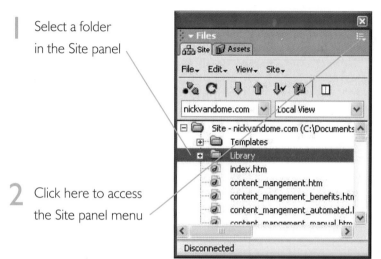

Once a folder or file type has been cloaked a red line is placed through it in the Site panel.

2 Click here to access the Site panel menu

3 Select Cloaking>Cloak from the menu to cloak the selected folder

Cloaked items can be uncloaked by selecting them in the Site panel and selecting Cloaking>Uncloak from the Site panel menu.

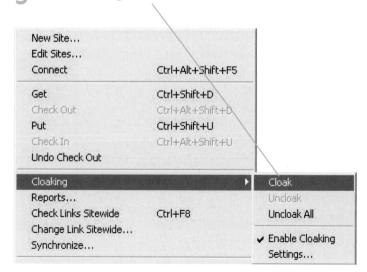

Checking files in and out

If you are working on a corporate website or an intranet it is likely that you will not be the only person working on the files that are in the site structure. If this is the case, it is important to know who is working on a certain file at a particular time. This avoids any duplication of work and ensures that the correct version of a file is uploaded to the live site.

If file checking in and out is not used, then it is possible for more than one person to be working on a file at a time, if it is in a shared environment. Unless you are the sole author of a website, it is recommended that file checking in and out is used.

Dreamweaver uses a system to ensure that only one person can be working on a file at a time, no matter how many other people there are in the team of Web designers. This is known as checking files in and out. For this to work properly, it has to be activated and then individuals can check files in and out as required.

Enabling checking in and out

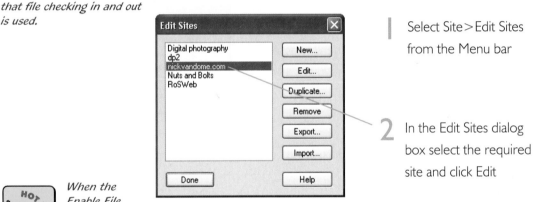

| Select Site > Edit Sites from the Menu bar

2 In the Edit Sites dialog box select the required site and click Edit

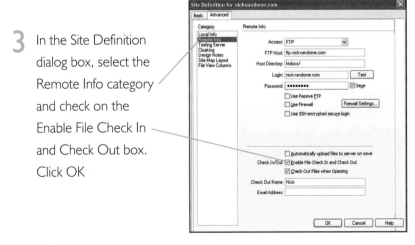

When the Enable File Check In and Check Out box is checked on, this activates another option, for adding the name that you want to use as identification for when you are checking files in and out. Make sure it is something that the rest of the design team will recognize easily.

3 In the Site Definition dialog box, select the Remote Info category and check on the Enable File Check In and Check Out box. Click OK

Checking files in and out

If you are working in a team of Web designers within the same site, you can check out files to prevent other people making changes to them while you are working on them. Once you have finished, you can then check them back in to make them available to the rest of the team.

When a file is checked out it is done so from the remote site. A read-only version is then placed in the local folder. The checked out version can be edited in the same way as any other Dreamweaver document.

1 In the Site panel, select a file in either the remote or the local folder (the one that will be checked out will be in the remote folder regardless)

2 Click the Check Out button

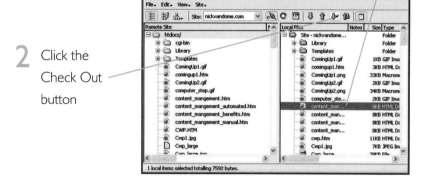

If a file has been checked out by someone else, it has a red tick next to it instead of a green one.

3 You will be connected to the remote site and the selected folder will be checked out. This is denoted by a green tick for any files that you have checked out. It is shown as being checked out in both the local and remote folders

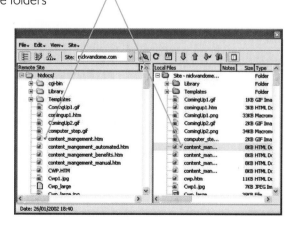

To check in a file so that other people can then work on it, select it in the remote folder and click on the Check In button. This should be done once you have finished making any editing changes and saved the file.

Synchronizing files

When you are updating and editing files and checking them in and out, it is easy to lose track of whether the most recent version of a file is in the local folder or on the remote site. Dreamweaver offers a solution to this problem, in the form of file synchronization. This automatically updates both the local and remote sites so that the most recent version of all the site files is placed in each location. To synchronize files between the local and remote sites:

If you only want to synchronize certain files, select them first in the local or the remote folder and then select the Selected Local Files Only in the Synchronize box of the Synchronize Files dialog box.

1 In the Site panel, select Site>Synchronize from the Menu bar

2 In the Synchronize Files dialog box, select whether you want to synchronize the entire site or only the files in the local site

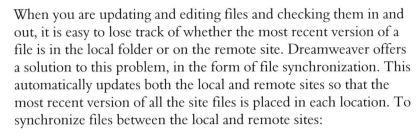

Once the synchronization options have been selected, Dreamweaver connects to the remote site to check the versions of the files there. Therefore, make sure your modem is turned on and your Internet connection is active when you want to perform any synchronization.

3 Click Preview to see the files that will be updated

If the latest versions of all files are in both the remote and local site folders then a message will appear stating this and saying that nothing requires to be synchronized.

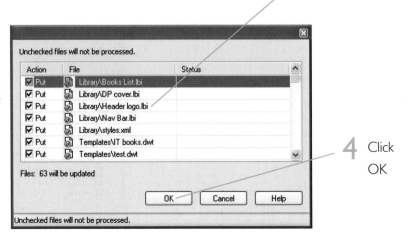

4 Click OK

Index

M

N

P